Cassandra Eason is a well-known author and broadcaster on psychic and spiritual experience, folklore and superstitions. She teaches different aspects of psychic development and is the author of several bestselling titles including *Psychic Families*, *The Mammoth Book of Ancient Wisdom*, *The Psychic Power of Children* and *Discover Your Past Lives*. Her books for Piatkus include *Angel Magic*, *Becoming Clairvoyant*, *A Complete Guide to Magic and Ritual*, *A Complete Guide to Psychic Development*, *A Complete Guide to Divination* and *Pendulum Dowsing*.

A complete guide to

FAIRIES & MAGICAL BEINGS

Also by Cassandra Eason

Angel Magic
Becoming Clairvoyant
Cassandra Eason's Complete Book of Tarot
A Complete Guide to Divination
A Complete Guide to Psychic Development
Pendulum Dowsing
The Modern-Day Druidess

A complete guide to

FAIRIES & MAGICAL BEINGS

CASSANDRA EASON

piatkus

PIATKUS

First published in Great Britain in 2001 by Piatkus Books Ltd
This paperback edition published in 2011 by Piatkus

Copyright © 2001 by Cassandra Eason

The moral right of the author has been asserted.

A CIP catalogue record for this book
is available from the British Library.

ISBN 978-0-7499-5499-4

Typeset by Action Publishing Technology Ltd, Gloucester
Printed and bound in Great Britain by
CPI Mackays, Chatham ME5 8TD

Piatkus
An imprint of
Little, Brown Book Group
100 Victoria Embankment
London EC4Y 0DY

An Hachette UK Company
www.hachette.co.uk

www.piatkus.co.uk

Contents

Introduction: Fairies – Myth or Spirituality?

'It was magic ... the whole sea was green fire and white foam with singing mermaids in it. And the Horses of the Hills picked their way from one wave to another by lightening flashes! That was the way it was in the old days!'

Puck in *Rewards and Fairies*,
RUDYARD KIPLING (1865–1936)

Fairies have been described in mythology and actual experience in almost every culture and age. They are as varied in their forms and attributes as nature itself: gentle and ethereal, magnificent beings of light, hideous black forms with eyes like glowing coals, golden-haired maidens, withered crones, a shadow in the grass, a rustling of leaves when there is no wind, the ripple of sunlight or moonlight on water.

THE MODERN LEGACY

In earlier times, benign fairies were regarded as invisible but integral members at the family hearth, working on farms, at looms or in workshops while the human owners slept. They were appeased with offerings, entreated to bring blessings and good fortune on the home. In contrast, malevolent spirit beings were held responsible for the failure of crops and the disease and death of animals, rather than attributing such disasters to the hand of fate or human inefficiency, and such spirits were to be repelled with charms and incantations.

Belief in fairies declined in many parts of the Western world from the late seventeenth century onwards, as a result of the Age of Reason, of Darwinism and of increased industrialisation and urbanisation in the nineteenth century. In an environment removed from nature fairies became fictionalised, sanitised, the province of children or saccharine sentimentality.

But in rural places where Celtic influence remained strong, the little people have never ceased to hold sway. Even today few people in Ireland will build houses on fairy paths, lines which connect ancient hilltop forts, and many still leave out milk or even whiskey at night as libations.

The case of the Cottingley Fairies, in 1918 (which became

the subject of a major film, *Fairy Tale, A True Story*, in 1997),
recaptured public interest in these spirits at a time when the
massive death toll of the First World War made people desperate to believe in life after death and in the power of goodness
over evil. For though, as will be described in Chapter 3, all but
one of the Cottingley fairy photographs were discredited,
Frances, the younger of the two children involved, insisted to
the end of her life that the remaining photograph was genuine
and that the rest had been faked only to prove to disbelieving
adults that there really were fairies in the glen.

At the beginning of the twenty-first century, because we
have caused so much damage to the planet through pollution,
destruction of the ozone layer and deforestation, nature
essences or spirits are once more entering our consciousness
as symbols of the need to recognise the sacredness and spirituality of the earth and to work with, not against, natural forces.
A Wiccan tradition known as the Faerie Faith has become
increasingly widespread, especially in America, acknowledg-
ing the joy and spontaneity of the fairy kingdom as a focus for
dynamic spiritual connection with the inner fey. Wicca is one
of the major forms of modern witchcraft in which both the
Goddess and God forms are recognised, usually with more
emphasis on the Divine Feminine principle.

In lands whose natural beauty is still largely unspoiled,
belief in fairies remains strong. Iceland covers an area of
nearly 40,000 square miles (104,000 square kilometres) but
has a population of only 275,000, most of whom live around
the coast. It is a leader in modern technology, with more
Internet connections per head of population than anywhere
else in the world. But people here still accept the existence

of elves, dwarves, trolls, light-fairies and the hidden folk who inhabit rocks.

At the time of writing, road authority contractors are planning to move rather than destroy a cracked grey boulder known as Grasteinn, said to be owned by dwarves, that blocks the expansion of a highway on the outskirts of Reykjavik. Viktor A. Ingolfsson, a spokesman for the road agency, commented: 'When Native Americans protest against roads being built over ancient burial grounds, the US listens. It's the same here. There are people who believe in elves and we don't make fun of them.' Magnus H. Skarphedinsson, who teaches folklore, says that in such projects: 'If you ignore the hidden people, the cost of construction doubles or triples. Everything goes wrong. The workers get sick. The machines don't work.'

ARE FAIRIES TRUE?

Scientists and rationalists remain unconvinced about the existence of such insubstantial creatures fluttering round the laboratory as light beams or shape-shifting as moths. They cannot be pinned down long enough to be measured or tested, or to answer a questionnaire on their partiality for acorns or fondness for mortal lovers.

The belief in a parallel universe that may exist independently of our own and yet occupy the same space runs counter to the concept that we humans are the only sentient life in the universe. Travellers in the modern world rarely walk across lonely moorlands with only the light of a lantern or sleep under the stars in the shelter of ancient stones or a grove of trees – and no self-respecting fairy would linger on the subway late at night or frequent a neon-bright service station.

However, children still see fairies even in towns and, with their psychic vision, indigenous peoples are teaching city-dwellers to see the spirits of the stones and flowers and trees. And despite the advances of science, we do not yet know everything about our own world. Each day new species are found that defy our wildest imagination, and species that we thought had died out are rediscovered flourishing in some remote forest without expert intervention. As I write, for instance, *The Times* newspaper of 19 August 2000 reports that an Amazon Indian tribe thought to have died out in the 1920s has reappeared in Brazil's Acre state – 250 Naua descendants have been found in the Serra do Divisor National Park.

As late as the 1700s real fairies in the form of white-robed Druidesses were living in France, on the misty Ile de Sène off the coast of Finisterre in Brittany. Other remote places, such as Cornwall, Ireland, Wales and vast tracts of Scandinavia, were cut off from the rest of the world for hundreds of years until better roads and new railways were built in the late eighteenth and early nineteenth centuries. Local legends dating back before that time tell how members of ancient orders of priests and priestesses, in an unbroken tradition going back to pre-Celtic times, would come to fountains and groves, recognised haunts of fairies, under cover of night. There they would accept offerings of fuel and food while conducting secret rites and offering healing to the local population.

It is only very recently that the old fire festivals of Beltane or Walpurgisnacht (May Eve), Lughnassadh (the beginning of August) and Samhain (Halloween) have ceased to be celebrated by ordinary people in forests and on hilltops. However, even in cities like San Francisco pagan associations are re-establishing these traditions as celebrations to which the community is welcomed.

These fire festivals date back to Celtic times or even earlier and were seasonal celebrations of the cycles of the crops and of the animals. Beltane was the beginning of the Celtic summer and was a fertility festival in which young people made love in the fields to symbolically increase fertility of humans, cattle and corn. Lughnassadh was the first corn harvest in which the last sheaf of corn represented the corn god, who willingly offered his life that his body might be buried and bring new life to the land. Samhain was the beginning of the Celtic New Year and winter, a time when cattle were purified before being either kept in barns for the winter or slaughtered for winter meat. It was also time when the living family were welcomed back from the fields and dead relatives were invited to share the warmth of their hearth.

Alien encounter reports, too, are demonstrating remarkable similarities to medieval tales of fairy abductions. Many of the less benign aliens bear striking similarities to goblins and gnomes.

There is more than just one explanation for the existence of fairies. A number of recognised fairy forms, such as the flower fairies of the country garden, the wild water kelpies of the Scottish lochs and the djinns of desert places, reflect the nature of the terrain they inhabit and perhaps draw power from it. Indeed, all the possible explanations contribute to our understanding of a spiritual force that can be sensed if not seen in places of natural beauty. Some fairies may be folk memories of goddess-worshipping peoples of small stature who have died out or been absorbed into a conquering race; whilst others may be spirits of the forgotten pagan deities, transformed in legend into opalescent beings akin to angels, who in traditional lore control the weather and harvest.

The number of fairy legends and reported sightings close to ley lines and sacred sites suggest that these special places may provide the power for abstract forces to be manifest as personalities that reflect various ages and cultures, such as the white ladies of lakes and fountains, the medieval courtly fairies, the shadowy moss wives of the groves, and the earnest grey-bearded Germanic dwarves who smelt magic metals. Ley lines are believed to be psychic energy lines that run beneath the earth throughout the world, connecting sacred sites that were built in places where the earth power was felt to be strong. Earth or fairy lights are most common over places of concentrated natural energies, and geological explanations provide only half the story.

ANIMISM, THE RATIONALE BEHIND FAIRIES

Animism is the belief that everything in the natural world — flowers, trees, lakes, mountains, crystals and so on — is endowed with a spirit. It was the root of early religion and has survived among indigenous peoples such as the Australian Aborigines and the Native North Americans. Corn and other grain was traditionally regarded as containing the spirits of fertility. The superstition of touching wood for luck, to appease the tree spirits, probably predates even the Druids in its origins.

Among the Native North American peoples, each herb and plant is said to give off a special aura and they were sometimes adopted as power totems. Some Australian Aborigines derive their origins from plants. In the Classical Greek and Roman tradition, dryads and hamadryads were tree nymphs – hamadryads were said to die if the tree in which they lived was cut down. Some of these nymphs fell in love with gods and humans and sometimes married them – or scorned them. Neo-paganism has restored this sense of interconnectedness in the modern world, and so contact with the spirits of nature has once more become recognised as a potent source of spirituality. Neo or new paganism is an umbrella term for a number of modern religions, including Wicca that believe in the sacredness and the interconnectedness of all forms of life: plant, mineral, animal and human. *Paganus* is Latin for country dweller.

Children are often acutely aware of these natural essences. Lilian, a clairvoyant from Berkshire in England, was very ill as a child during the 1940s and used to watch nature spirits during her months away from school: 'I got very close to nature and began to be aware of the presences in the countryside around me. I started to use my willpower to bring out the essences of these presences. I was aware even then that other people did not have time to see.'

Fairies, Good or Evil?

Throughout history fairies have tended to be amoral, rather than on the side of either angels or demons. For while there are fairy folk associated purely with destruction and others with helpfulness to humans, many natural essences can be alternately benign and malevolent. Like a wind that can change from a gentle breeze to a gale, it is a difference of degree rather than of quality. On the whim of a fairy, a mortal might be rewarded with gold or tricked into following unsafe paths across marshland – just as a child playing with a computer game may decide to let the electronic hero win or be destroyed.

Our ancestors did not expect their gods and goddesses always to be pure and noble, and neither do indigenous peoples. So fairy folk may be a catalyst for change, a reminder of unpredictability and of a life consisting of darkness as well as light, loss as well as gain. They can make us see the need to accept responsibility for our own shadow side rather than projecting it on to other people, the forces of fate or, in folk tradition, the fairies.

FAIRIES IN THE TWENTY-FIRST CENTURY

We are beginning to recognise once more what our ancestors knew psychically as well as psychologically. Far from being mere childhood stories, and for adults an escape into fantasy, the rich mythology of Fairyland mirrors issues that have confronted people for generations: fortune versus misfortune, fate versus free will, perfection and imperfection in the changeling phenomenon, illusion and the nature of objective reality, different time scales, the existence of parallel dimensions and the duality of human nature. For example, there is a split in folklore between ethereal and fairy queens who bring healing and summer flowers, and the hags of Scotland, Ireland and Wales who are a form of the ancient Crone Goddesses of death, transformation and rebirth.

Glamour

The term 'glamour' is derived from the Scottish word 'glaumerie' meaning magic. Fairies can create illusions to convince a young man that he is making love to a beautiful maiden and not an ugly old hag, and can create magical feasts and fairy gold that turn to dust in the morning light.

Why should fairies use glamour? Traditionally one purpose was to capture mortal brides or youths for the fairy queens, or to steal human babies and to exchange them for fairy offspring known as changelings.

As recently as 1894 in Clonmel, County Tipperary, Ireland, a young woman, Brigit Cleary, was tortured and killed by her husband because he claimed she was a witch changeling. He argued unsuccessfully that his wife had been spirited away by the fairies and substituted with a block of wood enchanted with glamour that appeared to act and speak like his wife.

Some people even believe that fairies are becoming more visible, as they were in pre-industrial days, because we need a reminder of the consequences of a consumer society in which instant gratification has assumed undue importance – the danger of being seduced by our own versions of fairy gold and glamour. By using different fairy forms as a focus for ritual, clairvoyance and psychic development, we can explore different aspects of our own nature and strengthen our connections with untamed creatures and wild places as a source of personal power.

Some fairies may indeed be projections of our own fears and feelings. But of course there may also be whole nations of fairies who have their own path of evolution and are as fascinated by us as we by them, and who may argue whether or not we exist. They may regard us as alien life forms and so be hostile, especially if they see us despoiling the planet they must share with us – perhaps a reason for the increase of poltergeist activity in recent times.

What is most surprising to sceptics is that fairies from different parts of the world and from different ages have common characteristics in legends with no apparent geographical connection. Perhaps also the fact that so many people have reported fairy folk in actual sightings, extending back many hundreds of years, would suggest that fairies may indeed possess objective reality. It may be pretentious to assume that fairies exist because we need them, or that if we do not believe in them they cannot exist.

Are we looking to the skies for signs of other life in the universe when it may be much closer – in the woods, the seas and the mountains? Have we sacrificed the clairvoyant vision of our ancestors by focusing on the material and the immediate, filling our lives with noise and pollution? Do *they* believe we have gone away, or wish we would?

I have been researching fairies over a number of years and made many visits to fairy places. For me the most fascinating aspect is the growing realisation that the cosmos is far more complex, far more uncertain but maybe as exciting as we believed it to be when we were children. So this book is about the hows and whys and wheres and ifs of the fey dimension and its inhabitants that have come down in folklore and folk memory as an important part of our own heritage, a microcosm of our larger world and yet one that is in some ways spiritually far more powerful. As well as being an almanac of fairies, this book looks at the significance of fairies to people in the past and present and in the ecosystem; and through a series of related activities it suggests ways in which we can use fairy power as a focus for and amplification of our own innate magical energies to enhance the world of reason.

EXERCISE: CONNECTING WITH THE ESSENCES OF THE NATURAL WORLD

In the early morning or evening, when it is very quiet, go alone to a place where there are trees and flowers and bushes growing wild.

- Take a notebook, a pen and coloured pencils.

- Examine the different plants in turn – thistles, trees, bushes, gorse, wild flowers, grasses and so on.

- As you touch each, close your eyes and allow in your mind's vision an essence to take shape. It may not be what you would expect – it may not even be a recognisable form, but a swirl, a series of brightly coloured lights, an old man or woman or a young child. You may hear words in your mind.

- Record each fairy form immediately afterwards, not worrying about your artistic ability but capturing the mood and the movement. Some may evoke a few lines of poetry or a song.

- If any essences feel unfriendly or unwelcoming, pass on quickly.

- When you have finished, sit and allow the stillness of the place to suffuse your being, becoming in your mind the gentle breeze moving the grasses or the bird song, so that you are no longer separate, an observer, but feel like a fairy would.

● Afterwards, pick up any litter, scatter a few seeds or leave a little food for the birds as part of the cosmic exchange.

● Later, look at each of your recollections and see if a name for the essence suggests itself. Look through the A–Z of World Fairies at the end of this book or one of the suggested books in the Useful Reading section, or enter 'faery' or 'fairies' on your Web Browser and search for illustrations of different kinds of fairies. You may discover that your image, name and description are remarkably similar to that of a recognised fairy form.

● Place your notebook by your bed, reading it again before you fall asleep. You may dream of your fairies.

● Some people keep a special blank notebook for their fairy work – many of the great fairy illustrators began in such a way.

● Whenever you go to a place of natural beauty or magnificence, try to spend time quietly connecting with it and recording the essences.

● Tune into the auras in your garden or even those surrounding any greenery or flowers on your balcony. The humblest office pot plant will have its own spirit – this will need special nurturing and frequent outings to your garden to restore natural energies that can grow weak as a result of electricity and noise. Remember that the same is true of your own spirit, for humans are not really town creatures but are meant to roam free.

CHAPTER ONE
The Origins of Fairies

When the first baby laughed for the first time,
the laugh broke into a thousand pieces and they all
went skipping about, and that was the
beginning of the fairies.

Peter Pan, J M BARRIE (1860–1937)

airies or faeries are frequently regarded in either angelic or demonic terms, but they are essentially different. No one knows when a belief in fairies began, but the legends of indigenous peoples whose traditions survived for thousands of years in song and story tell of encounters with the fairy kingdom. For example, one of the principal deities of the New Zealand Maoris is Tangaroa, the God of the Oceans and of fish, sea fairies, mermen and mermaids.

According to Native American belief, humans are but one of several races inhabiting the Earth. There are also the

Standing People (the trees), the Stone People (the rocks), the Four-Legged People (the animals), the Plant People (all that grows), the Feathered People (the birds) and the Crawling People (the insects). Along with the Two-Legged People (men and women), all are equally sacred and interdependent in the great hoop or wheel of existence. Indeed, as the most recent creation, man is regarded as having much to learn from the older and wiser forms of life. In such a view fairies, as the essences of plant, tree and stone and as spirits of wind, water, fire and storm, predated human and even animal life. Humans have created forms for these spirits that resemble our own, but in miniature so that we may try to contain their power within the world we believe we have been given to rule.

In the Westernised world, theories of the origins of fairies have therefore reflected different cultures and ages as explanations for energies that were experienced, but were not easily categorised.

CHRISTIAN VIEWS OF FAIRIES

One of the most intriguing theories is that fairies were once mortal, but were punished for the sins of Eve. An Icelandic legend, perhaps Christianised by missionary monks in the eleventh century who saw fairies as part of the pagan world they sought to eradicate, says that Eve was washing her children when God spoke to her. In fear, Eve hid the children she had not yet washed. When God asked if all her children were present, Eve said they were. This angered God, who declared: 'As you have hidden your children from my sight, so shall they for evermore be hidden from yours.' This is said to explain why children can see fairies who presumably never grew up (shades of Peter Pan), and the desire both of mortals to see and interact with fairies so as to restore the lost kinship and of fairies themselves to live close to the mortal world and sometimes share it.

Fallen angels and other theories

A popular view that still persists in countries of Celtic culture is that fairies are fallen angels driven out of Heaven with Lucifer, but not sufficiently evil to be cast into Hell. It is sometimes hypothesised that they did not fight against God but remained neutral, and when St Michael closed the gates of Heaven against the rebels they were left outside. A fairy's station in life was determined by where he or she fell to Earth, so that for example those who fell into water became undines or water nymphs. This accords with what is called the naturalistic theory, that fairies reflect the nature of the terrain they inhabit, an aspect which was briefly explored in the Introduction. Certainly there are descriptions of fairies from Ireland and Brittany as tall shining beings.

But not all Celtic cultures follow this story. In Manx tradition, it was said that 'Themselves', as fairies were called to avoid the taboo of naming them directly, were the souls of those drowned in Noah's Flood.

From medieval times fairies were demonised by the

Catholic Church and later by the Puritans. At the trial of Joan of Arc in 1431, fairies were cited as part of the evidence against her. It was claimed she had practised rites round an oak known as the Fairy Tree when she was a young woman. In fact, that particular tree had become a shrine to the Virgin Mary and the girls wove garlands in her honour, an example of the mingling of old and new religious traditions that was common among ordinary people of those times.

The old gods

Another theory states that the fairies are former gods and spirits of wise pagans such as Druids whose power dwindled with the coming of new faiths, especially Christianity. This accords with an ancient belief that a deity can only be powerful as long as he or she is worshipped.

This is certainly the most common origin cited for the *daoine sidhe*, the underground fairy court of Ireland, who are said to be the former gods of the Tuatha de Danaan, described as beings of light, the Shining Ones, the Shimmering Ones and the Ancient Ones from the Land of Youth.

According to the Breton writer Hersart de la Villemarque in 1839, the Corrigans were female fairies who were formerly great princesses but, refusing to accept Christianity, were cursed by God – or, rather, the early Christian saints. The Bretons also believed that some were the souls of Druidesses, condemned to do penitence for ever. They were seen most frequently near fountains next to dolmens, 'in lonely places from where the Virgin Mary, who passes for their greatest enemy, has not yet chased them'.

As mentioned earlier, some of these were actual Druidesses who survived until the eighteenth century, offering healing and medicine to people in return for food and money – hence the power of healing attributed to fairy women. They may also have acted as midwives for local women, and in Brittany the practice of setting aside a room for the fairies next to any birthing chamber survived into the nineteenth century.

The deities of the Old Religion that were not demonised were transformed in folklore and legend into fairies, and thus became less of a threat to the newly established religion. The Mother Goddess survived in myth and secret worship as the Good Fairy, Fairy Godmother or Queen of the Fairies.

But in some ways this was counter-productive. The legends of the old gods, diminished in size and status to fairies by the priests and monks who wanted to destroy their hold on popular consciousness, kept alive the ancient pantheistic form of religion that embraced darkness and light, good and evil, benevolence and destruction. These powerful fairies are described in Chapter 9.

DESCENDANTS OF THE NEOLITHIC PEOPLES

Another theory that accords with the explanation of the diminished gods contends that fairies were descendants of the small, dark, Neolithic people who retreated to remote areas, especially islands, to escape from Iron Age invaders. In

Ireland these little people were called the Feinne; in Scotland and Cornwall the Picts (after whom pixies may have been named); and in Scandinavia the Finns and Lapps.

Historically, it would seem that in Ireland the Tuatha de Danaan, the ancient hero-kings whose people worshipped Dana the Mother Goddess and were famous for their magical powers, were conquered by the first Gaels (the Milesians). They may have fled to the hills, islands and other remote places that in later mythology became Tir na n'Og, the Land of Youth, the Celtic Otherworld, a land of light. This might be reached through doorways on grassy fairy hills or beneath lakes or the waves. The Isles of the Blest and the subterranean places were linked by tunnels.

In these remote lands, the dispossessed tribes could continue the hunter-gatherer way of life from their round earth homes, using their flint-tipped arrows and flint knives and spears, sometimes known as elven or fairy shafts. They carried with them the tradition of worshipping the Goddess. Because they became so elusive, tales grew up of their fairy kingdom and powers of invisibility; and because of their closeness to animals, it was believed that they could shape-shift into deer or birds. Their defeat by the metal sword-wielding invaders is reflected in their legendary fear of metal and especially of iron.

As late at the thirteenth century there were tales of men marrying fairy brides, small fey women who were remarkably advanced in herbal medicine, and it was said that through intermarriage clairvoyance had entered the Celtic races centuries earlier. The association between fairy mounds or round barrows and the round huts of these early peoples gave rise to beliefs that fairy people lived beneath the earth.

Once the small, dark-haired and brown-skinned races had died out or intermarried, their exploits and magic became romanticised in mythology and fairy tales. Some of these people may have been captured and worked as servants or even slaves for the invaders – hence the image of the household brownie who would mend roofs and harvest crops in return for a dish of cream and honey.

Of course, these historical theories are not proof that fairies do not exist, but explain the way our ancestors tried to make sense of the powers that were close to the animistic beliefs of indigenous peoples, and which could not fit into a monotheistic religion. Theirs was a world of misty moorlands, silent pools and wild mountain passes where strange voices could be heard on the wind and shadowy beings could be perceived, and it did not fit easily with the angels and demons who came to represent the spirit world and whom, as late as the seventeenth century, magicians (including popes and high churchmen) tried to invoke and bind to their bidding. It is no wonder that many ordinary people kept allegiance to the more homely fairy folk.

THE SCIENTIFIC THEORY

Professor Howard Lenhoff of the University of California has put forward a theory that the little people owe their origins to Williams syndrome, a hereditary condition that affects one in every twenty thousand births. Williams children are known for their unusual faces: they have full cheeks, large eyes, small upturned noses, wide mouths, tiny chins and oval ears. They grow slowly and many remain small. They have difficulties in some areas of learning but are gifted in others, such as music, and have a remarkable empathy with people. It may be that people with this condition entered folk memory as little people and especially as changelings.

But, ingenious though such connections are, and valuable as genetic deformities are in explaining, for example, the popularity of the changeling theory into the nineteenth century, they do not account for fairy beings who are neither docile nor elfin. Examples include the warlike Bokwus of the north-western American spruce forests, who paint their faces and wait near fast-flowing water to drown fishermen; and the brigand Phookas, black Irish goblins who can shape-shift into bulls, wild dogs or wild ponies.

SPIRITS OF THE DEAD

The more frightening aspect of fairies stems from the belief that they are spirits of the restless dead. From throughout Ireland and Britain come accounts that link the fairies to the dead. For example, Finvarra, Fin Bhearar or Finbarr, mythical king of the *daoine sidhe*, had as his entourage a vast host of both the recent and ancient dead. This may partly be linked to the fact that Bronze Age burial mounds have been excavated on sites regarded as fairy forts.

But not all fairy hills are tombs, and the church of St Michael on Glastonbury Tor in Somerset was built over a natural hollow hill, regarded as an entrance to Fairyland, with the intention of blocking it off. Legend records that an earthquake caused the church to collapse and only the tower, the shape of a pagan symbol of power, remains.

Links with the Celtic Otherworld also strengthened the connection between fairies and the souls of the dead. In Cornwall the Old People are, according to legend, the souls of pagans who died before Christianity and were neither good enough for Heaven nor bad enough for Hell. It was further thought that they would shrink over the centuries until they became as small as ants and would finally disappear.

In Brittany, it was believed until the beginning of the twentieth century that those who died resided with the fairies and at night would return to their former villages and homes to continue their work and daily lives while mortals slept. On 1 November, the second day of the ancient Samhain, the beginning of the Celtic New Year and the Christian Day of the Dead, dead souls were welcomed to the family hearth. On this day spirits were believed to congregate at Mont St Michel, on the borders with Normandy, at the Isle of the Dead. As late as the 1900s in the hilltop village of Pleine-Fougères 10 miles (16 kilometres) from Mont St Michel, at funerals the coffin would be carried to a slope overlooking the bay and turned to face Mont St Michel before being interred.

The Celtic Otherworld was not like the Christian Heaven, but a place of feasting, music and laughter in which some awaited rebirth – a land in which the old gods still ruled and where heroes could become deities. However, some who dwelled there had never, it was said, lived as mortals nor ever would. Heroes might visit during their life-times for wisdom, and King Arthur is there awaiting his call to save the land once more. Though the Otherworld might be accessed through a hill or over a sea, it was regarded as present within and not separate from the world. However, it had a different time frame from mortal time, another simi-larity to Fairyland (see p. 36). It was not until the medieval churchmen conjured up their visions of the fiery pits of Hell and demonised fairies that this darker aspect clouded the issue, dividing the dead into the good who went to Heaven and the tormented who rode with Finvarra.

ALIENS AND FAIRIES

On 10 December 1954 at a place called Chico-Cerro de las Tres Torres in Venezuela, some dwarf-like hairy beings, no more than 4 feet (1.2 metres) tall, were reported to have landed in a spacecraft and attacked two hunters. From France, too, came accounts of goblin-like creatures from space attacking people, mocking them and dancing around. In 1955, in one of the earliest reported direct encounters with extra-terrestrial beings in the USA, five tiny goblin-like creatures with dark, wrinkled skin, large ears and eyes were seen by a family outside their Kentucky farm. The farmer shot at one of the creatures, but the bullet fell off it with a metallic sound. When a family member went outside to investigate, one of the creatures touched his hair with a silvery hand. These extra-terrestrials became known as the Hopskinville Goblins.

Early Australian Aboriginal cave drawings depict celestial beings with antennae. The Aborigines also displayed advanced knowledge of aerodynamics when they devised the boomerang, which is thousands of years old and yet identical to a modern aircraft wing. Is this extra-terrestrial knowledge or a gift from the fairies? And are fairies, especially in view of their apparent ability to fly, extra-terrestrials who were interpreted by our ancestors as nature spirits?

Alien abductions also share characteristics with fairy kidnappings – the need to reproduce with humans, and the fact that alien abductions operate outside the material time frame. Except in the case of the noble, tall, alien Nordics, who resemble the statuesque opalescent fairies, the entities are usually known as greys. Greys are extra-terrestrial beings believed to be smaller than the average adult, with greyish skin pigmentation, huge oval heads, staring almond eyes and spindly limbs. It is said that they are eager to discover more about and breed with humans, in order to modify their own genetic makeup and ensure the survival of their race. They not only share physical characteristics with goblins, but, like fairies, are often amoral, curious about humans rather than showing any empathy with them and as capable of behaving with cruelty as with kindness. Fairies have their magic rings, whilst aliens are implicated in the sudden appearance of crop circles. With both fairy and alien encounters lights may appear in the sky. Indeed, some modern UFO abductees locate the places to which they were taken by extra-terrestrials as under the ground or beneath the water, where there was brilliant light – the Celtic Underworld, no less.

Conversely, the modern world may be perceiving fairies as extra-terrestrials and the earth lights of fairy mounds as UFOs. Perhaps the fairy glamour, the power of enchantment, is causing us to see fairies in terms of the twenty-first century? Perhaps fairies have updated the images they portray? All this is, of course, mere speculation. And in a sense all the explanations for fairies may contain grains of truth. For if there is a parallel universe whose inhabitants possess the powers of shape-shifting, invisibility, creating illusions and moving in and out of time, we can be sure they are not simple creatures.

EXERCISE: CHOOSING A FAIRY POWER FORM

We all have our own concept of fairies. For some it is a strong wind blowing a field of corn, for others a flower fairy complete with gossamer and wings, a powerful being of light, or a wise brown gnome in a woodland or garden.

Like any other symbol of power, protection or challenge, a fairy guardian can form a focus for your own innate power and wisdom, amplified by the aspect of nature that is repre-sented by the fairy. If you select a fairy form now, it may serve for a few days, weeks or months or during a particular period of joy, challenge or crisis. Because fairies can shape-shift, your guardian may appear as an animal or bird or seem to reside in a tree in your garden. There may, for example, be a wild bird who always appears when you are sad or anxious, or a particular fragrance in your garden or on your balcony that is amplified at times when you are especially sensitive.

- If you sense a spirit in a tree that has special power for you, find a fallen branch of the same wood and carve with a penknife a shape to represent the guardian.

- Alternatively, buy a statue that expresses what a fairy is to you. You will see one by synchronicity (meaningful coincidence), perhaps in an unusual place when you least expect to. I found my blackthorn fairy guardian in a dusty old bookshop.

- If you see or sense a flower fairy near a particular species or display of flowers, keep a pot of the living plant in your home.

- Hang a string of silver bells near an open window for a sylph of the air. Alternatively make a water feature, drop crystals in a bowl of water or add to fish to represent your water fey. Add weeds or water plants to the water if s/he is a creature of the reeds.

- If your essence is manifest as a bird or animal, craft a clay form of your power creature. You can also make your own fairy from clay, if possible found naturally.

- Try to spend a few moments each day quietly holding your symbol, smelling the flowers or rippling the water.

- Then close your eyes and see the essential form taking shape, as you did when you touched the different plants in the exercise on p. 13.

- You may at first perceive a flash of colour or light shimmer or a sudden rainbow. Allow any words to flow through your mind.

- Your guardian may appear at other times as a sudden fragrance when you least expect it, or in a vivid dream.

- In time the power will accumulate, so after a few weeks you have only to close your eyes at any time to connect with the power.

- If your guardian seems hard to contact or after a while loses potency, wrap the symbol in white silk or, if it is a natural symbol, return it to the earth and begin with a new guardian form.

CHAPTER TWO

Who Are the Fairies?

Fairy elves,
Whose midnight revels by a forest side
Or fountain some belated peasant sees,
Or dreams he sees, while overhead the moon
Sits arbitress.

Paradise Lost, JOHN MILTON (1608–1674)

airies are found in mythologies throughout the world. Especially rich in fairy lore are Brittany, Cornwall, Ireland, the Isle of Man, Scotland and Wales, the Mediterranean lands, Germany, eastern Europe and Russia, Scandinavia and Iceland. These fairy traditions – and some believe the fairies themselves – travelled with the colonists to the USA, Central and Southern America, Australia, New Zealand and South Africa. It was most notably the *bean sidhe* or banshees and the *bean tighe*, the fairy housekeepers, who journeyed with the descendants of ancient Irish and Scottish families to the New World. Immigrant fairies co-existed or even mingled with indigenous nature spirits.

In places where a traditional way of life prevails, even in cities and apartment blocks, fairies still form an integral part of the traditional structure. Since the change from Communism, Russia has seen an influx of consumer goods and cosmopolitan restaurants in its large cities. But for the majority of people in the former Soviet Union life changes little, no matter who is in power. In rural places people work the land in the same way their ancestors did. Russian elves, *domovoi* and *domovikha*, live in cramped, utilitarian apartments and help with household tasks as well as in country dachas as they have for centuries. These creatures with pointed ears, who latterly lived in cellars, now inhabit dark corners of apartment blocks.

Dolya, a tiny old lady who brings good luck, is often associated with the goddess/fairy of fate and lives behind the stove. When she is angry she becomes Nedolya, the shabbily dressed crone of bad fortune. Like the Albanian Fatit, who appears at the side of a crib three days after birth and ordains a child's fortune, Dolya manifests herself either as a grey-haired old woman or as a beautiful young one at the birth of a child.

Because Helena Blavatsky, the founder of the Theosophical Society ('theosophy' is derived from the Greek *theos* (god) and *sophia* (wisdom) and is rooted in the belief that all major religions are derived from one original, universal religion), was a *sedmitchka*, which means she was born in the seventh month, she was said in her native Russia to be able to control supernatural beings. On the night of her birthday, the servants would carry the little girl around the house and stables while sprinkling holy water and repeating magical incantations to appease the family *domovoi*.

But where technology rules, it is harder to connect with the magic. So adults as well as children seek the magic of J. K. Rowling's Harry Potter stories or Tolkien's world as a reminder of what is buried in their memory. Indeed, it might be said that if you inhabit a place where there is no room for magic, it is not good for people either.

NAMES THAT MUST NOT BE SPOKEN

The word 'fairy' or 'faerie' comes from the ancient French *faes*, derived from Latin *fata*. It was first used around the thirteenth or fourteenth centuries to describe spirit beings who had been central for hundreds of years in the oral folk tradition of many lands.

'Faerie', 'fairy' or 'fayerie' originally meant a state of enchantment or glamour, the power of illusion, reflecting the power of beings who might bring blessings or curses, and an ambivalence towards such beings. It was fear of angering the fairy folk by speaking their name that led to their being given a variety of euphemisms that might, by a process of magic, attract only their benevolence. In Ireland they were known as the Good People and in Scotland as the Good Neighbours; in Wales, the Tylwyth Teg or Fair Ones were referred to as

Bendith y Mamau, which means Mothers' Blessing. The latter terminology was invoked to avert their tendency to kidnap children. The Grey Neighbours was the euphemism used by the Shetlanders when speaking of the trows, the small, grey, goblin-like trolls whom they so feared. The aim was to remind these creatures of their obligation to act in a neighbourly fashion and desist from eating the locals.

THE LITTLE PEOPLE

Though some of the more aristocratic fairies have been described in the fallen angel genre as being as tall as humans or even loftier, fairies were generally diminutive. They varied in size from small, sturdy children like the Spanish winged *jimaninos* and *jimaninas* who travelled to Mexico and South America with the early colonists to the *abatwa* of southern Africa who are so tiny that they live in anthills. Chapter 1 mentioned the concept of fairies as diminished gods or tiny races of people: Cornish pixies, for instance, are believed to be Picts who have continued to diminish in size and will eventually disappear.

Another possible explanation for the size of fairies may be found in the primitive idea of the soul as a miniature replica of man himself, which emerged from the owner's mouth in sleep or unconsciousness. If its return was prevented, the person died. Therefore if fairies are spirits, whether disembodied entities or mortals who died or were captured, it would follow that they also were tiny. But of course fairies could really just be naturally small.

ARE FAIRIES IMMORTAL?

It is sometimes said that fairies do not have souls, for which reason they use glamour to shape-shift and then seduce mortals, seek human wet nurses for fairy children or exchange their offspring with mortal infants in order to acquire a soul for their descendants.

Fairies may, according to legend, exist for hundreds or even thousands of years. For example, an Irish giantess called Garbh Ogh was said to have lived for many centuries and to have hunted the mountain deer with a pack of seventy dogs, all of whom had the names of different birds. When she chose to die, according to an old Celtic verse, she piled around herself stones in a single cairn, 'set her chair in the womb of the hills at the season of the heather-bloom and breathed no more'.

When fairies do die, it is said that they cease to be. For example, the grandmother mermaid in Hans Andersen's story of the Little Mermaid explained: 'We sometimes live to three hundred years, but when we cease to exist here, we only become the foam on the surface of the water ... we shall never live again; but, like the green sea-weed, when once it has been cut off, we can never flourish more. Human beings, on the contrary, have a soul which lives forever .... It rises up through the clear, pure air beyond the glittering stars.'

Of course, that is a Christianised point of view that runs counter to the Celtic Otherworld belief described in Chapter 1. What is more, accounts of fairy funerals which suggest that fairies do not live for ever might mark the ending of a specific body or the death of fairies with mortal blood.

There are many inconsistencies in fairy lore, since everyone from bard to child perceives the fairy kingdom through subjective eyes and those of their own age and culture. It seems that questions of immortality are no more clear-cut in the fairy kingdom, perhaps because the issue is so emotive that it is hard for us to understand concepts that may not fit into conventional Heaven/Hell, life/death categories.

FAIRYLAND – ANOTHER PLACE OR ANOTHER DIMENSION?

One theory is that Fairyland exists within this world, but that fairies occupy a different vibration, wavelength or dimension, so that contact is like using a short-wave radio that may crackle, fade and then suddenly become clear for a few brief moments. As mentioned in Chapter 1, children and those who are naturally clairvoyant or become psychically evolved can see fairies, just as mediums communicate with people who have moved on through death to another dimension.

At certain places there seem to be natural doorways

between the dimensions, a theme explored in the Narnia stories by C. S. Lewis (see Chapter 4). Natural entrances to Fairyland are especially prevalent at places where earth energies are strong (see Chapter 7).

For example, at Carnac in Brittany the dolmen placed at the end of the rows of more than a thousand stones at Kermario, which means 'village of the dead', is said to be an entrance to Fairyland. It was built around 3500 BC and predates the stones. Even on a bright May afternoon, with coach parties crowding around the stones that are now fenced off for ecological reasons, I felt the otherworldliness of the place. Only minutes later my husband John and I were lost in the deep mist that can suddenly shroud the landscape, reducing all to silence.

Time in Fairyland

Accounts from throughout the Celtic world suggest that time in Fairyland differs from that in the mortal world. Stories abound of people who were away for what they thought were days, and return to find their friends and family old or dead.

One of the most common stories is of the bridegroom abducted on his wedding day by an envious fairy queen. Brides were originally surrounded by up to ten bridesmaids similarly dressed and the bridegroom by the same number of groomsmen, so that the fairies would not know whom to seize.

Invariably the bridegroom is bedded and feasted by the fairy queen and returned home (having impregnated her at what was regarded as his peak of potency, his earthly wedding night). However, several years or even decades have passed in the mortal world, and in the worst cases only a very old man or woman recognises him.

In one variation a man may agree to stay with the fairy queen, but wish to return to see his family. He is given a magical horse and told that he must not dismount; when he does so to greet a former love, he crumbles to dust.

The key to crossing the time dimension seems to be eating fairy food or entering into a sexual relationship so that the enchantment is absorbed. Falling asleep on a fairy hill, beneath a hawthorn or in a fairy ring creates a more limited period of enchantment that lasts for a year and a day, but to the dreamer seems only a few minutes.

The entrance on Glastonbury Tor in Somerset was guarded by Gwynn ap Nudd, the White One, fairy king and Lord of the Otherworld. From the Tor he led the Wild Hunt (see Chapter 8) at Samhain and on stormy nights was accompanied by the white hounds of the Otherworld. Sometimes associated with King Arthur, he lived in a palace within the Tor, sitting on a golden throne, surrounded by fairies wearing silks of all the colours of the rainbow.

Confusion arises because some bards portray the fairy world as an actual place (rather than a state akin to that experienced in shamanic travel or the dream planes) to be literally reached across the sea, beneath a lake or by entering a physical door in a fairy hill. Some have given a specific location to Tir na n'Og, which under various names remained the symbolic home of fairies right through to the medieval Arthurian legends.

Bards attempted to locate the way to this earthly paradise west across the sea. Islands with ancient sites were associated with the Isles of the Blest, as the Otherworld was sometimes called. Mont St Michel, already mentioned, was one. The Isle of Arran between Scotland and Ireland was also identified as Annwyn, one name often given to the Otherworld. It was the home of the Cauldron of Plenty, which many scholars believe was the inspiration for the Holy Grail.

One of the best descriptions of the Celtic Otherworld is found in the Welsh poem 'Preiddeu Annwyn'. It was to Annwyn that the hero bard Taliesin, son of Cerridwen, Welsh Goddess of Inspiration, went in search of the original Holy Grail. There are three regions, the first of which is the land of the Silent Dead. Here the Lost Ones are contained within a glass fort known as Caer Wydyr or Nennius. This would accord with descriptions of gold and crystal palaces in Fairyland.

The second realm is Caer Feddwidd, the Fort of Carousa, ruled by Arianrhod, the Goddess of Time, Karma and Destiny. Here a mystical fountain of wine offered eternal health and youth for those who chose to spend their immortality in the afterlife.

The third realm, the most divine, has become known as Avalon, meaning the Vale of Apples, and is the sacred Isle of Arthur. Only the most spiritual, or those who had made great sacrifices for the benefit of others, could enter here. King Arthur was its most famous inhabitant. Avalon was located at Glastonbury and even today, though Glastonbury Tor is now land-locked, many people, myself included, have remarked on the distant water all around as they climb up the spiralling path to the peak of the hill. Remains of lake villages, built perhaps as early as 4000 BC when the region was still covered by water, have been found in the vicinity.

In Celtic tradition, the Well of Wisdom or Connla's Well in Tipperary in Ireland stands at the centre of the Otherworld or the Land of Eternal Youth, and all other sacred wells and springs throughout the world are believed to be tributaries. On the hazel tree hanging over the water were the ever-renewing nine nuts of poetic art. The nuts would periodically fall into the water and be eaten by salmon, Celtic fish of knowledge and mystic inspiration, who sent the husks floating down the five streams that flow from the well, so endowing other sacred waters with an ever-flowing source of wisdom. For this reason the hazel became known as a magical tree.

TIR NA MBAN, THE LAND OF WOMEN

Perhaps the most mystical Isle of the Blest was the realm ruled over by beautiful fairy women and their queen (origi-nally the goddess Arianrhod). Here time stood still and the women would delight any travellers who reached the island by chance or on a quest with love, feasting and poetic or musical inspiration. In return, the fairy women were impreg-nated. Men had the option of remaining with their new consorts and gaining immortality or at least several hundred years of erotic bliss. However, most sailed home to become great bards or poets. Medieval myths concerning ladies of the lake draw on this tradition, and it is not surprising that such a land remained a male fantasy through many generations.

A rather earthier version is told concerning Mont St Michel. Here the Druidesses who worshipped the god Belenus or Bel in pre-Christian times had magic darts which, it was said, they threw at the waves to calm tempests. When the villagers on the mainland wanted to ask favours of these priestesses, they chose a handsome young male virgin as emissary. The Druidesses led him to a cave in the rock where he went through a series of voluptuous rites. After several days the young man returned to his village covered in cockleshells – the Druidesses sewed another cockleshell on to his clothes every time he brought them to ecstasy.

However, it seemed that the land of beautiful women might materialise anywhere, and tales of seductive Breton Corrigan women are remarkably similar. In an updated version of the legend, Emile Souvestre, the nineteenth-century folklore collector and author of *Le Foyer Breton*, tells how Jean Kerlof of Sulniac spent the night of Easter near the Roche aux Fées at Caro. He saw tall, beautiful Corrigan women, dressed in white and luminous, dancing in the moonlight. He was so afraid that a lock of his hair turned white. No details of his participation in rites is given.

Of course, even here the power of glamour is at work, for in other sources the Corrigan is described as a beautiful maiden by night but a hag by day. Legend says that if a mortal would accept her in both aspects she would be transformed permanently into her lovely form.

But maybe we should not go all the way down the Celtic Otherworld track. If fairies are, as is sometimes suggested, creatures below the angels but above the mortals, then fairy realms may exist separately from the Celtic Otherworld and the two have become entwined because of the similarities of description. Of course, we cannot easily separate out the layers of myth and history; and if we seek to analyse too closely, or to apply literal boundaries to a non-material reality, we can end up applying the wrong criteria and either adapting fairies to our preconceptions and needs or dismissing what may be an essential part of the archetype of magic as the stuff of children.

DIFFERENT KINDS OF FAIRIES

Fairies are classified in different ways that have considerable overlap. There are the powerful fairies, sometimes associated with the deities and wise ones of old: the fairy goddesses/ queens who are often regarded as aspects of the Triple Goddess (an ancient form of the goddess, frequently associated with the Celts, based on three cycles of the Moon that correspond to maiden, mother and wise woman/crone); the enchanters, like Merlin; and enchantresses such as Morgan le Fey, who was of fairy descent and one of the Ladies of the Lake (see p. 198–203). Merlin was regarded as an archetypal figure who, it is said, was reincarnated through mortal form or took possession of a willing body, usually an Archdruid. For example, the Celtic bard Taliesin was said to have accepted Merlin into his body in later years so that he might guide Arthur.

Then there are the darker creatures of fairy tale and nightmare: giants, trolls, djinn and goblins. Separate again are the nature spirits, devas, elementals, nymphs and merpeople, although other fairies – pixies, for example – do help to tend nature. These fey forms have their own chapters.

In this section I concentrate on what are regarded as pure fairy types: the noble fairies as portrayed in Shakespeare's *A Midsummer Night's Dream*, who live in courts, feasting and dancing and controlling the seasons, and the tinier fey folk such as elves and pixies, who live together in troops and are usually expert at music and crafts. Finally there are solitary beings: they either hide from mortals, like the leprechauns who jealously guard their treasure from prying eyes, or help in homes or on farms – for example brownies, who may have a family, but only congregate with other fairies on festivals and at the fairy markets. Each kind has its own history, mythology and lore.

Fairy courts are a feature primarily, but not uniquely, of Celtic lands.

Sidhe or *sith*

This is the name for fairies in Ireland and the Highlands of Scotland; they are portrayed as a beautiful, noble race who are as tall as humans or even more statuesque, and resemble them. They are of the fallen angel/diminished deity genre. It is difficult to ascertain how far the courtly aspects of the *sidhe* have been imposed by medieval French Grail legends, in which fairies played an important part, and by later works such as Spenser's *Faerie Queene*, written in honour of Queen

Elizabeth I, with Fairyland as a microcosm of courtly England under Gloriana – Elizabeth herself. This aspect will be explored in Chapter 10.

The *sidhe* live in subterranean fairy palaces of gold and crystal and are endowed with youth, beauty, joy and great musical abilities – all the gifts of the Celtic Otherworld. Maybe given the Christian slant of their existence, their greatest regret is said to be that, though they rule nature, they cannot return to heaven from which they were once cast. This is supposed to explain their ambivalence towards humans and their desire for mortal consorts.

Fairy Borrowings and Fairy Gifts

In earlier times the exchange of favours between mortals and fairies was mutually beneficial. Mortals offered milk to farm fairies and guardians of the land, and fish to sea-dwelling beings. On the Isle of Lewis in Scotland fishermen still pour a barrel of ale into the waves on Halloween, so that the sea spirit Shony will bring them a good catch throughout the year.

Until the mid-twentieth century the Scottish islanders poured libations of milk into hollow stones for the fairy crone Gruagach, guardian of the herds. At night, in homes throughout the Celtic world, fires were made up and food and water left out for the fairies. In return they would help around the house or farm, ensure a good catch or a rich harvest and assist with spinning, weaving or shoemaking. Any tangible gifts left by the fairies, such as money or ever-filling grain tubs, were kept a secret or the blessing would cease.

The *daoine sidhe*

The most famous fairy court was that of the *daoine sidhe*, the former Tuatha de Danaan of Ireland, the people of the Mother Goddess Dana. According to myth, they were driven out between 3000 and 1000 BC and became in folk memory the fairy people – gods yet not gods. The Tuatha de Danaan were credited with building the megaliths of Ireland which are still seen as gateways to the world of fairy, and they were the guardians of the original Grail treasures.

There are various legends throughout history of mortals stealing fairy chalices. A crystal chalice of incredibly exquisite workmanship, now in the Victoria and Albert Museum in London, was supposedly taken from the fairies by a butler of the Musgrave family in Cumberland. The cup was retained by the family for generations and brought them great luck.

Finvarra or Fin Bheara, who ruled the fairies of the West of Ireland and was perhaps their most noted king, loved hurling and was never beaten by a mortal at chess. His queen, Oonagh, was described in true Victorian style by Lady Wilde, who collected accounts of fairy folklore in Ireland, as having 'golden hair sweeping to the ground, clad in silver gossamer glittering as if with diamonds, that were actually dew drops'. In spite of this ethereal beauty, Finvarra was obsessed with mortal women who, overpowered by the music of Fairyland, were spirited away to live there with him for ever. He was also said to have a second queen, Nuala. Other maidens seduced by Finvarra's music danced all night with him and in the morning found themselves on a fairy hill far away, possessing knowledge of love potions and of magic – and sometimes a fairy pregnancy.

The *daoine sidhe* were famed for their music, and many aspiring musicians would sleep on a fairy mound in the hope of being transported to Fairyland to be endowed with the gift of fairy music-making. But this was not without a price, for, although the musician often went on to acquire fame and fortune, he remained under fairy enchantment and would have to return to Fairyland when summoned – many did disappear mysteriously after several years of success.

It is easy to see how a beautiful young woman who could attract any man as though by magic and perhaps ended up pregnant could all too willingly attribute her situation to a night with the fairies. Fairies were a prime candidate for blame as well as praise in mortal affairs – but that is not to dismiss astral or dream encounters with Finvarra, or those who did indeed hear music with their clairvoyant ear in places of great earth energies and who reproduced the sounds of enchantment. Indeed, much Irish music claims fairy origin.

The Seelie Court and the Unseelie Court

The Seelie or Blessed Court represents in Scotland the almost angelic air spirits who were reputed to ride the winds, overseeing mortal affairs and offering help when needed and dispensing justice. Like the Irish *sidhe*, they had underground palaces of gold and crystal.

In contrast the Unseelie Court, also referred to as the Slaugh or Host, were considered to be the unblessed dead or those who had been cast from the Seelie Court for misdemeanours (though not for kidnapping mortal lovers, which was acceptable in fairy morality). Their appearance is likened to a huge dark cloud passing overhead on the night wind, and they were blamed for disasters in the mortal world. Unlike the Seelie Court, who took lovely maidens and youths, the Unseelie Court kidnapped less desirable humans to swell their numbers. Many disappearances of minor criminals and vagrants may have been attributed to this myth rather than to earthly elimination processes.

Trooping fairies

This is the name usually applied in Celtic lands to less noble groupings of Tuatha (tribes) of fairy beings. They may or may not have their own king and queen, and fall under the rule of the higher courts. On fairy festivals they come together with other tribes for celebrations.

In non-Celtic lands, they are any fairies who live in groups. They are associated with fairy rings and with green hillsides, fairy paths, woodlands and meadows. Sometimes they are regarded as controlling a particular woodland or expanse of water, or as caring for the environment in that area. They are smaller than the noble fairies and almost inevitably have a trickster element, though they also reward favoured mortals at whim. Many of these trooping fairies are regarded as elf-like people who practise crafts, and are mischievous rather than malevolent, challenging the status quo and causing sufficient chaos to prevent stagnation.

In Gotland, the largest of the Swedish islands in the Baltic Sea, with a population of about sixty thousand, small beings called *Di sma undar jordi* live under the earth. They wear grey or blue clothes with small caps, probably like the pixie hat – originally hoods worn by the local people – and are said to be the size of small children. These beings leave flattened circles in fields, like mini-crop circles, in the centre of which mortals still leave coins, milk, linseeds, beer or salt to prevent or cure illness.

The elven kingdom

In Viking and Germanic tradition the courtly aspect was less in evidence, though there were elven kings and queens who possessed great magical and prophetic ability. The Alfs or elves of Scandinavia and Germany were, like the Seelie Court, divided into two categories, higher and lower, light and dark elves, though there was not so strong a connotation of evil in the dark elves.

In Viking lore, the Ljossalfs or light elves lived in Ljossalfsheim or Alfheim, one of the nine worlds that made up the universe on the top level of the World Tree, above the world of Midgard where humans lived. This land was close to the realms of the gods and so the light elves can be regarded as higher forms of fairy life, closer to the *sidhe*. However, relatively little of the lives and organisation of the light elves has been recorded in myth, so it can be assumed that they played little part in mortal lives. Ruled by the fertility god Frey, they were rarely seen by mortals.

Swartalfs, the dark or black elves, inhabited Swartalfsfheim, which extended from Midgard to Helheim, an underworld realm on the lower part of the Tree. The Swartalfs were said like the dwarves to be skilled craftsmen, making treasures for the gods, and were also expert at spinning. In the Brothers Grimm's fairy tale *Rumplestiltskin*, it was probably a dark elf who promised to spin straw into gold for a maiden in return for her first-born child. The dark elves got their name because their skins turned dark from the soot of their forges.

Mound-alfs, a sub-group of the dark elves, are more akin to the traditional elves seen on Earth since they dwelled in Midgard, the land of mortals. The merry elf figure is a sanitised version of these beings, who could be helpful or malicious according to whim, and could use elven music to enchant mortals. They were said to be the spirits of the dead and so were found near burial mounds. They are reported to appear at the full moon and to dance all night. Their mesmeric music can cause trees and stones to dance, and any mortals who hear a song called 'The Elf King's Reel', will be forced to dance until they drop, unless the strings of the musician can be cut or the mortal can seize the fiddle and play the tune backwards. 'The Elf King's Reel' is named after the powerful Elf or Erl King of Germanic legend, who is a harbinger of death and is discussed in Chapter 8. Like dwarves, elves cannot appear during daylight without risking destruction, hence their image of creatures of the night.

Pixies

The most famous of the true trooping fairies are the pixies or piskies of Cornwall, Devon and Somerset in England, and of Scotland. Their origin is unknown. Said to be no larger than a human hand, but shape-shifters who can increase or decrease their size, they are described as having translucent wings, oversized heads, pointed ears and pointed noses. Their caps are made from foxgloves or toadstools. Tricksters, they steal horses at night to ride them across the moors while they twist and tangle their manes. Pixies also lead humans in circles, using the powers of illusion to create paths and then cause them to disappear, calling down patches of mist alternated with dazzling sunshine, creating lights at night to suggest the presence of houses that are not in fact there, and making marshland appear solid. Under their invisible guidance, mortals become hopelessly lost – hence the expression 'pixie-led'.

Until recent times in remote country areas, farmers would leave out buckets of water at night so that pixie-mothers might wash their babies. Milk was also left for them to drink and the hearth was swept in case they ventured indoors to dance at midnight, the magical hour as night turned to the new day.

The name 'pixie' is, as mentioned earlier, derived from the tiny pre-Celtic peoples who lived on the north-eastern coast of Ireland, in Scotland and parts of Cornwall, and who were eventually driven into marshland, woodlands and underground by metal-wielding invaders. It is said that pixies fear both iron and salt because the Picts did not possess these commodities, but the invading Celts did.

The pixie tribes in Cornwall may have continued to live under the protection of surviving priestess cults and local people who came to value their herbal and midwifery skills. Knowing the marshlands so well, they may have acted as boatmen for the priestesses. It is said that because they worshipped the old ways they must remain spirit beings until Judgement Day.

Pixies, like the Picts, were famed for their work in gold, silver and bronze. Pixie dust, gold and silver sparkles left where they tread, is a relic of this attribute and certainly graces the appearance of most fairies, regardless of type, in Disney films.

Dwarves

These are mountain dwellers associated with Germany, Switzerland and Scandinavia, and may be relics of a small race famed for its mining and metalwork skills and so forced to work in mines by the invaders. In Viking tradition they inhabited Nidallvellir, a realm on the lowest level of the World Tree. They are described as short, bearded, powerfully built, old even from childhood and are master craftsmen and magicians, fashioning magical swords and armour and extracting precious gems from the earth. They appear only at night, as it is claimed that even a single ray of sunlight can turn them into stone, perhaps because the original dwarves worked so long underground that their eyes could not bear the light.

There are many tales of these magical creatures. The most famous is of Alvis, a dwarf whose name means all-wise, who was promised Thrud, the daughter of the Thunder God Thor, as payment for the weapons he created for the gods. However, Thor told Alvis that he needed to prove by a test of knowledge that the suitor's wisdom compensated for his lack of height and beauty. Thor prolonged the test until sunrise and so Alvis was turned to stone. Another Viking legend tells how Freyja, Goddess of Beauty and Love, agreed to sleep with the four dwarves Dvalin, Alfrig, Berling and Grerr in return for a dazzling necklace that eventually became the Milky Way.

Solitary fairies

There are said to be several reasons why fairies live separately from their own race. Some, it is said, were banished from the fairy court for various misdemeanours. Into this category falls the Manx Fenoderee, a generic name for a spirit akin to a brownie who is said to work for the farmers of the Isle of Man. He was banished from the Ferrishyn, the small Manx trooping fairies, and deprived of his beauty because he missed the Autumn Equinox festival to be with a mortal girl.

Another reason for being solitary was to avoid human contact. There are many tales of the Irish leprechaun foiling the attempts of mortals to steal his gold. Leprechauns are described as small old men dressed in green, sometimes with a leather apron, wearing buckled shoes and three-sided hats, a symbol of the ancient Irish Triple God.

Each leprechaun is said to possess a crock of gold. If a mortal, alerted by the sound of the hammer, catches the leprechaun and holds him fast, he will promise to reveal the location of the gold. However, the leprechaun is an expert trickster, and if the human takes his eye off him, even to blink, the leprechaun is gone. Should this fail, the leprechaun has two leather pouches. The first contains a magical silver coin that always returns to the purse no matter how many times it is given in payment. The second contains a gold coin which the leprechaun will give to the mortal to buy his freedom, but this coin will turn into leaves or ashes. So while the greedy human is admiring his new-found wealth, the leprechaun disappears and the crock of gold remains undetected.

Household fairies

These are usually solitary, although in the case of ancestral spirits there may be several guarding a home. The most famous ancestral spirit, the *bean sidhe* or banshee, is described in Chapter 9. However she has an alter ego, the benign *bean tighe*, a fairy housekeeper or domestic fairy godmother and as such a personalised representation of the Mother Goddess. Like the banshee, she is attached to a specific family rather than to the house.

Her name means 'woman of the house' and she guards children, especially during the night, as well as pets and the hearth, traditionally regarded as the centre of the home and refuge for both living and deceased family members. She also helps with household chores and supplements the maternal role. *Bean tighes* would also reside in the homes of village wise women with whom they felt great affinity, though this could lead to accusations of witchcraft during times of perse-cution, especially if an old woman had an immaculate house and hence, it was claimed, fairy help.

The Spanish, Central and Southern American *duendes*, described as middle-aged women dressed in green, also attach themselves to a household, but unlike the *bean tighe* the *duende* is motivated by envy. She cleans only for her own comfort and tries to displace the family. *Duendes* can act like poltergeists, throwing crockery and moving furniture to scare away the mortal residents. Exorcism is said to be ineffective as they are very tenacious.

Brownies

The most famous household fairies in Scotland and England are brownies. Welsh brownies are known as the *bwbach* or *bwca*. So called because of their brown skins and clothing, brownies complete household tasks left unfinished by mortals during the day, though they prefer to work outdoors. They will assist with building work (but only wooden structures), bake bread and repair broken tools, and bring good fortune when they adopt a home. Sometimes brownies live as part of an extended family and several may make a home in human dwellings. However, they do not live in troops as such.

In Finland the less benevolent male brownies are called the Tomtra. They torment residents into becoming tidy, and if the humans fail to smarten up their act their Tomtra will leave and take away the family luck. Regrettably, Tomtras are not available by mail order to chivvy recalcitrant teenagers! The Tomtra keeps Thursday as his sacred and rest day. He expects food and comfort all year and gifts at Christmas. An expert fiddle player, he can be heard playing during the nights of the old festivals.

Boggarts were regarded as the negative counterparts of

brownies, especially in the north of England. A brownie angered by his adopted family, perhaps by forgetting his milk and honey or speaking in derogatory terms of his or her work, might be transformed into a boggart. Boggarts are ragged, dark and covered with hair. They hide tools, poke babies to make them cry and even cause minor accidents.

EXERCISE: EXPLORING FAIRY QUALITIES WITHIN THE SELF

It has been said that we identify with fairies because they express qualities within the human condition that we admire or fear. Whether you accept the objective reality of fairies or regard them more as personified essences and qualities, it can be helpful to explore the personalities of both benign and malevolent magical beings, adopting the strengths even of the less benevolent fairy forms as a catalyst for positive change or assertiveness in the face of injustice.

- Make a series of cards, each about one and a half times the size of a playing card, in white or pale colours. On each one write, draw (or use pictures from the Internet or postcards) the names of different magical beings.

- On each card write a few words to describe these beings' salient qualities, for example the attention to detail and perseverance of the dwarves, the nurturing qualities of the *bean tighe*, even the acquisitiveness and challenge to the status quo of the *duendes* if your rights are being eroded.

● You can use the fairy forms mentioned so far, adding new cards as you read more or access additional sources of fairy material, such as the A–Z of World Fairies on p. 219, or any of the books listed on p. 243. Twelve fairy cards will suffice initially, but you can make as many as you feel relevant, which may be fifteen, fifty or more.

● Leave one side of the card blank.

● Select the fairy card whose qualities you know you will need at a particular time. Sleep with it under your pillow or carry it in a special purse or sachet during the day.

● Alternatively trust your intuition, especially if a matter is not clear, and each morning select a card at random from the shuffled set, arranged clockwise face down in a circle. You may find holding a pendulum over each card in turns helps your selection. The pendulum will feel heavy, pull down or circle clockwise over the right card. You will soon learn your individual positive pendulum response, even if you do not regularly use one.

● Once you have finished reading this book and have made up cards to reflect the fairy qualities that attract you, choose a core set of no more than thirty fairy beings that are most relevant to your current life and select a daily card from these.

● At times when you have a major change or decision in your life, select two or three cards from your entire collection, again placed face down in a circle. The first card will clarify the issue, the second indicate the strengths you will need, and the third an unexpected source of help. If the cards reveal challenging qualities these will clear inertia in others or unblock personal fears that may keep you from acting decisively or moving forward.

CHAPTER THREE

The Evidence for Fairies

'There are fairies at the bottom of our gardens'

Fairies, ROSE FYLEMAN (1877–1957)

Chapters 1 and 2 have concentrated on the folklore surrounding fairies, although this was rooted in the actual experiences of men and women who had encountered them. Since medieval times researchers, especially churchmen, have recorded accounts of those who have seen, talked with or been abducted by fairies. These were treated like any other human experience, for fairies were an accepted part of life and until the late Middle Ages people were claiming fairy descent as they would any noble lineage. Even today some Scottish, Irish and Welsh families recall such ancestry.

FAIRY SIGHTINGS

While the majority of such fairy sightings are in country places, fairies have been seen in houses and gardens even in towns. Many fairy encounters in childhood are recalled many years later with great clarity and an awareness that the experiences were not, as the children had been told, imagination. As with many psychic experiences, they are of the flashbulb kind in which every detail is etched on the memory like a photograph – the same phenomenon that has people recalling precisely what they were doing when they heard of the death of the Princess of Wales or of the first Moon landing.

THE SECRET COMMONWEALTH

One of the most fascinating accounts of fairy life is given in *The Secret Commonwealth of Fairies, Fauns and Elves*, published in 1691 by Robert Kirk. Kirk was himself, it was claimed, abducted by the fairies a year later.

A Scottish Episcopalian minister in the parish of Aberfoyle, Kirk was also a distinguished scholar and linguist and a seventh son, hence said to possess second sight. That he did not claim this power may have something to do with his position in the Church. But he recorded the fairy traditions of his parishioners, accepting the existence of the fairy peoples and the ability of those with second sight to see and communicate with them.

His successor, the Rev. Dr Grahame, described how, as Kirk was walking one day on a hill known locally as Fairy Knoll, he had collapsed and apparently died. But it was rumoured that the fairies had been angered by the minister revealing their secrets and taken him away.

A few days after his funeral Kirk appeared as a wraith to his cousin, saying that he was a captive in Fairyland but would appear at the christening of his own child who had been conceived before his abduction. On seeing Kirk's ghost, the cousin should cast over its head an iron dagger as this would break the enchantment. Kirk's spirit did appear at the christening, but his cousin was so shocked that he failed to throw the dagger. Kirk disappeared, never to be seen again on Earth.

COLLECTING CASE STUDIES

Kirk's lore of the fairy people shows a startling similarity to accounts of the fairy races collected in Ireland, Scotland, Wales, Brittany and the Isle of Man two hundred years later by another scholar, W. Y. Evans-Wentz. He travelled through these regions in 1908–10, obtaining first-hand experience of people's beliefs. His extensive analytical work *The Fairy Faith in Celtic Countries* was published in 1911 and is still in print. He wrote:

> These experiences of mine lead me to believe that the natural aspects of Celtic countries impress man and awaken in him some unfamiliar part of himself – call it the Subconscious Self, the Subliminal Self, the Ego, or what you will – which gives him an unusual power to know and to feel invisible, or psychical influences. What is there, for example, in London, or Paris, or Berlin, or New York to awaken the intuitive power of man, that subconsciousness deep-hidden in him, equal to the solitude of those magical environments of Nature which the Celts enjoy and love?

One of Evans-Wentz's more intriguing accounts was collected from the area of Cuchulainn's mountain in Ireland. (Cuchulainn was a hero from Ulster in ancient legend; son of Lugh, the God of Light and the mortal Dectera he was regarded as a semi-deified solar icon.) An old woman visited the wife of Steven Callaghan, a local man, asking if Steven would leave uncut a hedge in which the fairies sheltered. Mrs Callaghan recognised the old woman as a person who had died giving birth many years earlier. The old woman visited the cottage a few nights later asking for food and was offered oatmeal, which she refused. The next morning the meal store was overflowing and Mrs Callaghan believed it was the fairy woman's way of showing gratitude for the preservation of the hedge.

Such fairy sightings still occur in Ireland. Melvyn, an

Archdruid living in County Laoise, told me that at the recent celebrations of Lughnassadh, the first corn harvest, he had seen some two dozen lights hovering and dancing over the outbuildings of his home. He related: 'It was as if someone had lit a giant sparkler and all the light beams were flying round.' Fairy lights are a common manifestation of fairies (see Chapter 7). The area in which Melvyn lives is one frequented by the wild Red Cap fairies, so named because of their brilliant scarlet hats. Farmers will stop their tractors and go home at 9.30 p.m. for fear of angering the little people.

MODERN RESEARCH: SCOTTISH BANSHEES IN AMERICA

I am indebted to Susan Shepphard, author of a number of books on divination and the paranormal and leader of the Haunted Parkersburg Tours in West Virginia, for information on the banshee who travelled with emigrants from Scotland and Ireland to America. She described a form of the Scottish banshee that I had not encountered before: 'The Scottish banshee, the *bean nighe*, gives a more menacing appearance. The Scottish banshee is dressed in grave clothes, with face covered by a veil while riding a dancing steed. Her age and features are difficult to make out but she appears to be an old crone.' Susan says that 85 per cent of West Virginia has families of Scottish and Irish descent, which may explain the number of banshee stories she has obtained.

One of the accounts she has researched is of a banshee who travelled from the Marr Forest, north of Aberdeen, to the mid-Ohio valley with Thomas Marr and his family. Marr moved to what was to become Marrtown in 1836 and after the Civil War obtained a job working as a night watchman at the toll bridge. Almost every night as he travelled to and from his work Thomas saw a robed and hooded figure on a white horse that would disappear as he approached it.

In February 1874 Marr's wife Mary was woken by the sound of footsteps. Outside the gate was a white horse whose rider wore a ragged veil. The rider told Mary that Thomas was dead. The shrouded woman and horse vanished as they reached the bend in the road.

Within an hour, the bad news was confirmed by one of Thomas's workmates. Some claim that it was the cry of the banshee lamenting his demise that caused Thomas to fall into the water and drown. The banshee appeared at other family bereavements and accidents, including Mary's death.

CHILDHOOD FAIRIES

Children have little difficulty seeing fairies, since their minds are not cluttered with logic or learning and they are sufficiently innocent to be open to other dimensions. Though fairies are associated primarily with nature and wild places, accounts of fairies have been given even by town children. I began researching this area in the late 1980s when I was trying to explore the psychic world of children for my very first book.

Quite independently, when they were young, Layla and her sister Rhiannon saw the same fairy in their bedroom in a council house in a northern industrial town. More than ten years later both girls are able to recall the details vividly. Layla, however, saw many other fairies. She told me:

'After being shown the pictures of the Cottingley fairies [see p. 73] in a book, I fully expected to see fairies. The fact that I lived on a council estate in Crewe rather than unspoiled woodland never entered my head. Fairies I wanted and fairies I got, although not the sweet gossamer creatures I'd pictured.

'I've always been a bit of a Nature child. I could potter about outside for hours. I was at my happiest when digging around in the muck, climbing trees or playing with bees (I used to let them crawl about on my hands and knees and never got stung).

'Nature was and still is endlessly fascinating to me. Every time something grabbed my attention I would see something more intriguing out of the corner of my eye. As my eyes flitted from object to object something strange would happen. Faces and forms would appear at the sides of my vision. They would appear only for a fraction of a second, and when I looked again they wouldn't be there.

'These faces and forms soon became familiar to me. I never thought to question them until years later. There were three distinct types, although I did occasionally see one I didn't recognise.

'The first type was the only one to worry me slightly. It

was two-legged, had no body and an eyeless head a little like a swan's beak (but it didn't seem to have a mouth, its head was just in that shape). Its legs were like horses' legs but much thinner. It was a cloudy grey-brown colour and much taller than me. It was so tall in fact that I'd never see the top and bottom half of it in one glance.

'My grandfather has two plaques on the wall. An artist friend cast them for him out of metal. They show two creatures very similar to what I saw in the woods. The similarity struck me one day and I asked him what the creatures were. He replied: "They're the things you see out of the corner of your eyes when you're alone in the woods."

'The second type was something I called "Tree Men". These were very strange indeed. For a second it would look as if somebody was entering or leaving through an invisible door on a tree trunk. The "somebody" would be very indistinct and transparent but definitely there. On one occasion a head poked out of a tree, saw me and promptly disappeared back inside.

'The third main type of fairy that I saw was closest to the butterfly-winged classic variety. It was small, about the size of a Barbie doll. It seemed very brittle, as if it was made of dry twigs. It would always be a lighter shade of the colours of the plants around it. Its eyes were huge and black, it had no nose, and if it had a mouth I didn't notice one. It would appear to be made out of a plant, with leaves and other foliage growing out of it. This fairy would always peek out from under something, although I did see one silhouetted against the sky once.

'My sister Rhiannon and I were chatting recently about the house we grew up in. We used to share the tiny front bedroom. We'd never spoken about this before, as she was so young when we lived there (she's seven years younger than me). The front bedroom was, as my sister put it, "weird". She shuddered to herself, and then went on to tell me a few strange things that had happened to her. She described the exact same thing I saw for several nights running. We both saw a tiny figure standing behind the curtain early in the morning.

'I remember this so clearly because I thought my mother had put a doll behind the curtain as a joke. I snatched the curtain back and there was nothing to be seen. Nothing to cast that sort of shadow on to my window, either. When the curtain fell back again it was gone. My sister said that she used to see it from her cot, and she told me that its hair seemed to be curly, in a kind of loose afro style which fitted in perfectly with what I saw.

'Lots of strange things happened in that front bedroom. Among these were a goblin-type creature running across the floor just as I was waking up, my name being whispered very loudly and distinctly behind me as I played in the otherwise empty room, and the constant feeling that there was some-body in the corner of the room (not a bad feeling, but not a very comfortable one either!).'

Rhiannon independently confirmed: 'I was the youngest, so anything about fairies was put down to my imagination. Stories usually resulted in "You're tired, go to bed", so I wasn't one to mention them. I say "them" – there was only one fairy I remember clearly. She looked like a doll with a big floating dress on. She had really huge, frizzy, shoulder-length hair and she was really pretty – very pale, though. All she did was pace up and down on my windowsill. The fairy looked at me once. I was really interested, but as soon as I got up to touch her she was gone.'

Felicity, a psychology student, remembers a field near her house in the country where 'as a child I used to see fairies in the long grass. They were typical fairies, a sort of greeny blue, the kind you see in Flower Fairy books. They used to talk to me. At the time I never told anyone. I was convinced they were real at the time. When we moved, after my parents divorced, there wasn't a field, so I didn't see them any more.'

Pat, who is now fifty years old, also saw fairies when she was about four, at the bottom of the garden belonging to the old lady who helped to take care of her: 'It was a big garden with a stream running at the bottom. The fairies were very tiny, dressed in pink gossamer, and used to play around by the stream. I told them my wildest dreams. They used to fly and hover with their tiny wings. I didn't tell anyone as I knew they would have laughed.'

Both Felicity and Pat found their fairies comforting.

Dr David Lewis, who lives in Shrewsbury in Shropshire, England, wrote to me about the magical creatures he saw as a child. They are akin to the earth lights described in Chapter 7. Fairies assumed the shape of birds quite frequently (see Chapter 5), but these creatures were somewhere between translucent figures and birds.

His father was appointed vicar of St Gluvias in Penryn, Cornwall, a land rich in fairy lore and sightings. 'St Gluvias had a large vicarage with about two and a half acres of wildly uncontrolled garden. Perhaps an acre of this was woodland copse with mature oak, ash, lime and other full-sized trees, dense brambles and dense undergrowth.

'I had as my bedroom a large first-floor room with a bay window looking directly towards the jungle. As I lay in bed in the darkness, I remember seeing the dark outline of the trees through the uncurtained window. In the trees I saw something which I called coloured birds. They were luminous creatures about the size of birds which moved occasionally through the branches. When they moved they left a trail of light, which soon faded. There were many of these birds through the field of view framed by the window, and always one or two in view.'

Fairy Rings

These circles of inedible mushrooms, often red with white spots, feature in all the best fairy tales. They grow naturally in Europe, Britain and North America and may spring up after rain.

According to folklore, they provide convenient magical circles where fairies and witches meet, dance and sing at night. A fairy ring in a field beside a house is a lucky omen.

Run nine times clockwise round the outside of a fairy ring to see fairies. Standing or sitting in a fairy ring at the full moon means a wish will come true. However, legend warns of interfering in fairy revels as one may be enchanted within the ring and forced to dance without stopping until dawn.

Fairy rings are closely linked with the ancient solar circle dances, which took place on the great festivals under the full moon.

Lilian, mentioned in the Introduction, was ill as a child and had to take a great deal of time off school, during which she roamed the countryside. Recently she described her experiences to me in greater detail. When she grew up she became a clairvoyant and healer, and she has the amazing ability to create wonderful gardens out of wilderness.

'I used to see fairies in our garden in Cheshire, but especially in the woods. They were semi-transparent and tiny with wings. I found myself looking at the little people in shadowy forms. They all looked different according to whether they belonged to a tree, a flower or a bush. The fairies from each species were the same colour and even the same texture, and would merge into a tree or flower.

'I used to sit and watch them for hours. They came in ones and twos and seemed friendly, but they got on with their own world of which I knew I was only a visitor – watching, not part. I never told the other children – I knew they would jeer. Over the years I have wondered if they were creatures that I invoked and they were already there, or if they were creatures that have always lived long before people and if we are frightening them away because of the way we treat the Earth.'

Most of the reports of fairy experiences that I receive are from girls. This may be because it is not macho to talk about fairies, but younger boys do see them. Andrew was only five when he told his mother about the fairies he had seen in the corridor at school: 'One had a green light and one had a blue light. They were the size of the palm of my hand. The fairy beings were in the centre of the light that became paler the further away the light was from them. They went by very quickly, one in front of the other, as if they were playing tag.'

Sadly, the more we impose artificial powerful stimuli, the

less the child's own psyche is able to respond to natural phenomena. But children are remarkably resilient, as I found when I interviewed a group of children about the Tooth Fairy.

THE TOOTH FAIRY

Even modern children subscribe to the idea of the Tooth Fairy, who exchanges teeth that have fallen out for money. One of my children was given a replica of a Victorian tooth pillow, embroidered and edged with lace, with a pocket for keeping teeth safe.

The Tooth Fairy is a character who goes back a long time, for it was feared that witches would wreak magic against children by using hair clippings or teeth that had fallen out. Such fears were natural in days of high infant mortality. It was also thought important to keep a child's first tooth and lock of hair throughout life, so that when he or she eventually died the spirit had a complete body; the teeth and hair were placed in the coffin. These ideas predate not just Christianity but all formal religion, and the Tooth Fairy is a form of the old Crone Goddess (see p. 180).

I talked to some children in a play group in Berkshire, England, about the Tooth Fairy. Five-year-old James assured me of their existence: 'There's Tooth Fairies. I have seen them, I think. My big brother is seven. He had three teeth come out when he was six. They came out on different days,

so the Tooth Fairy took them away on different nights.'
Three-year-old Nadia explained: 'If your teeth are wobbly,
the Tooth Fairy comes to take them and she makes another
grow and she gives you money, but it hasn't happened to me
yet.' Tamesin, aged seven, nearly missed the Tooth Fairy:
'Once I swallowed one of my teeth when I fell over. Damien,
my brother, said, "Oh, yeah", but I did. So I wrote a letter to
the Tooth Fairy telling her what had happened and put it
under my pillow and I still got my money.'

Dr Rosemary Wells, a lecturer at Chicago's dental school,
has opened a Tooth Fairy museum at her home in Illinois.
Sporting the title 'Tooth Fairy Consultant', Dr Wells says:
'Other fairies are just cute but the Tooth Fairy has a specific
purpose, helping children get through a tough time.' About
six hundred visitors a year come to the museum, by appoint-
ment, to see books, tooth boxes, craft kits, posters, video
tapes, T-shirts, and more than a thousand dolls. There is no
gift shop but children get a free fairy pencil, a plastic tooth
necklace and an educational booklet. The entrance fee is a
tooth fairy drawing, story or memory.

FRIGHTENING FAIRY CREATURES

But not all fairy experiences in childhood are so positive, and
parents who tell a child he or she is making it up can isolate
that child with the fears that have been awakened. Eleven-
year-old Jenny, who lives in Australia, recounted the

following experience that happened to her family while they were living in New Zealand. It is reproduced by permission of Daphne Plowman, Editor of the *Scottish Society for Psychical Research Journal*, and of Jenny's mother, Pauline, a gifted healer and medium.

Jenny writes: 'This true story happened in a quiet town called Whangarei in New Zealand. A little Maori boy woke one night and got out of bed to fetch a glass of milk. What he did not know was that watching him from the dark shadows of the door was a sinister form. He dropped his milk and turned round. All he saw was a pair of red eyes looking at him. The little boy ran through to his mum and dad's bedroom and started shouting and jumping round the room in terror. His mother calmed him and phoned a friend who is a Spiritualist, my mum Pauline.

'The next morning early my mum went to the Maori house to feel what was there. After some time and lots of prayers, my mother came home. Later that evening my brother Tod was lying on his bed. When he looked up he saw red eyes staring at him from the shadow of his wardrobe. Tod said it looked a bit like ET and was carrying a stone. It came over to the bed and deliberately dropped the stone in front of Tod. However, as the stone was spirit, it dropped straight through the bed, so the spectre bent down to pick it up.

'Tod screamed out for Mum and she came running through to the bedroom. The apparition ran behind the door when Mum came in. Tod saw the short black shadow and told Mum where it was. Mum turned round and saw it looking with its big red eyes. My mother said lots of prayers to get rid of it and finally a big hand came down from the roof and pulled it away. I think it was God's hand coming down and taking the spirit to heaven.'

The children were lucky that their mother was able to offer reassurance. There are similarities between the Maori spirit being and a goblin.

Ivy was not so fortunate, and suffered her fears alone. Though some might argue that the terrors were projections of Ivy's fears of sleeping alone, her adult mind rejected what would have been a logical conclusion, if not the true one. Indeed, she commented that the experience grew more real as she became older.

'I think I was about seven years old. I lived in a lovely house, high up in the hills, right on the Pennine chain. I never told my parents, because they would have said I was dreaming. But it is only these last few years I realised that those horrible, thin, wizened, toothless, spiky, grey-haired and some young ill-fed people were actually in my bedroom, which was built on to the Elizabethan part of the old farmhouse.

'They mocked and laughed and leered at me from behind the wardrobe and the washstand and came close to my bed. It was a kind of torment, as if something was trying to break me down.'

The situation was only resolved when Ivy's parents moved her to another room because she looked so ill and they feared her room was too cold. The experiences ceased.

THE COTTINGLEY FAIRIES

The most famous documented case of children seeing fairies, and the only apparently scientific evidence for fairies, is the still controversial and unresolved Cottingley affair. In 1917 cousins Frances Griffiths, aged eleven, and Elsie Wright, aged sixteen, claimed to have played with fairies in a glen at Cottingley in the Yorkshire Dales, and produced photographs which baffled the experts including the photographic company Kodak and Sir Arthur Conan Doyle, the creator of Sherlock Holmes and an ardent Spiritualist.

Frances had scribbled on the back of a photo sent in November 1918 to her friend Johanna back in South Africa, her former home: 'Elsie and I are very friendly with the Beck [stream] fairies. It is funny I never used to see them in Africa. It must be too hot for them there.'

One of the photographs seen by Conan Doyle showed a group of fairy-like figures dancing in front of a girl, the other a winged, gnome-like creature near a girl's beckoning hand. Some sixty years later, the cousins admitted that four of the photographs had been faked. They had made cut-outs of fairies and placed them in the glen.

But this is not the end of the story, because Frances said that they did take one genuine photograph. She told Joe Cooper, a psychic researcher and author of many books on the psychic including one on the Cottingley Fairies: 'It was a wet Saturday afternoon and we were just mooching about with our cameras and Elsie had nothing prepared. I saw these fairies building up in the grasses and just aimed the camera and took a photograph.'

Elsie insisted that all the photographs were fakes. But, like Frances, she claimed that there actually were fairies in the glen. The reason the girls had faked the pictures was to convince sceptical adults that the fairy folk really did exist.

Frances said she noticed the first fairy when she became aware of a willow leaf shaking, although there was no wind: 'I saw a small man standing on a branch, dressed all in green.' Gradually she began to see more and more of the elves, and in the summer of 1918 described how some of the fairies had wings and said that some would come very close. Like Lilian, who also saw fairies in her childhood, Frances realised that they belonged to their own world and that it was not her place to try to interact with them. Had she been making up the account, she would have described how the fairy folk spoke to her and played with her.

Indeed, the account is remarkably like that of many children. The problem comes when, as with any non-material phenomena, proof is demanded. Children have been caught faking a variety of psychic tests simply because they are unable to demonstrate under controlled conditions and therefore want to please researchers or to prove they were not lying.

ADULT EXPERIENCES

The adults who have described seeing fairy beings are all intelligent, rational people but are marked by a degree of sensitivity and insight that others lack. Vivien Greene, widow of the author Graham Greene, herself an expert on Victorian dolls' houses and not a fanciful lady but one of great culture, told me how she and her son had simultaneously seen a dark elf in his bedroom.

'When my son Francis was between three and four we were living in a house in Oxford. Francis was sleeping in a bed with drop-sided cot rails on either side. One evening I was putting him to sleep when he suddenly became distressed and told me, "I don't like the little man at the bottom of my bed."

'In a flash I saw momentarily what my son was seeing – the top half of an elf or gnome with a malevolent, spiteful face standing there. As quickly the creature was gone and there was just a pile of blankets at the end of the bed.'

It is very common for children and mothers to share experiences, for their psyches are not fully separated during the early years of a child's life and mothers often reawaken their own psychic powers when they have children. This may partly explain why women who are mothers may more easily see fairies in the presence of their children.

Julie, who is now a medium, told me that as a child she

lived in a house with a big garden. In the part of it where she played were little spirit friends who were like fairies. To Julie, they were not just pretend friends. In fact, she says that she has seen them in adult life, especially in a particular place in Devon. 'My own children have seen them too. Once when we were together we all saw them, when my son was nine and the youngest only about four.'

'What are they like?' I asked her.

'They are very fleeting, like butterflies, but not as small – about the size of squirrels.'

Mike, a journalist accustomed to sifting fact from fiction as part of his job, was walking home through the countryside of Cork in Ireland one night when he suddenly found himself lifted off his feet, propelled by unseen hands through the air and deposited in a thorn bush. When he returned to the home of the relatives with whom he was staying, they told him he had been attacked at the Fairy Corner where the little people were accustomed to play such tricks on lone travellers.

Flower fairies, too, may have been first painted because their creators had seen the essences of the natural world. At Pickmere in Cheshire, during the 1930s, Brenda had gone to a local Women's Institute meeting with a friend. On the main table was a vase of daffodils. Brenda noticed that one of the stems was broken and that a tiny winged fairy, like a butter-fly, was struggling to mend it. Brenda did not like to say anything, although they had consumed nothing stronger than tea. However, on the way home her friend asked if she had seen anything unusual about the flower, and they both admitted they had seen the fairy.

EXERCISE: FINDING THE FAIRIES

- Choose a time when you are on holiday or at a weekend when you are not rushed and can be in the countryside or a wild garden.

- At dawn or dusk, go out of doors and find a fairy place – a hawthorn tree, between two oaks, or near foxgloves, lilies of the valley or primroses which are their special flowers. You may even find a natural fairy ring – a circle of spotted toad-stools.

- Sit quietly in your fairy spot or in long grass, in a grove of trees or by running water.

- If you have children or can borrow a friend's or relation's under-five, ask them to come with you and explain that you are trying to find fairies. They will not think you at all odd, as children believe fairies to be a fact of life. They will also know instinctively the best places. You will be amazed at how still even a normally active child can sit when fairy-watching.

- Babies will often stare quite fixedly or gurgle at a particular spot in a garden, and if you can see with their eyes momentarily, the fey folk will be everywhere.

- Breathe in slowly through your nose the gentle green light of nature, and exhale through your mouth equally slowly and gently the dark light of doubt and the harsh light of logic.

● Let the essence come to you – a rustle of leaves, the movement of plants when there is no breeze, a beautiful butterfly that settles quite close, or a wild bird that lands next to you and views you quizzically.

● When you feel totally at one with the scene close your eyes, open them, blink quickly, and in that instant flash you may see your first natural essence or gain a fleeting impression rather than a full-blown vision.

● It is easy to get discouraged if you do not get the entire Seelie Court riding by at your first attempt, but it took you years to lose the clear vision of childhood and it may take equally long to regain it fully.

● So if you sense nothing, try again. If fairy sight still eludes you return to your breathing. You can visualise the colours of the pink and scarlet rays of the rising or setting sun in your inhaled breath. Visualising colours or essences is really no different from the pictures you created in your mind as a child. In any of the exercises, visualise the colours of your breath or the images of the fairy forms, and in time the actions will become spontaneous. This simply kick-starts the psychic processes that some of you may not have utilised since childhood.

● When you are ready, return home. Don't ask the child what he or she saw, but offer him or her a paintbox or a set of colouring pencils to re-create the scene.

- Let your own fingers return to the joys of colouring pictures, and you may discover that you and the child have created similar essences. If you went seeking fairies alone, play gentle music of nature (e.g. CDs of birdsong, rain forests or flowing rivers), and allow pictures to emerge in your head and on paper – or in words in poetry, song or story.

- Continue with your private fairy time in different settings. You will find the experiences restorative, and your intuitive awareness of the vitality within the natural world will increase.

- You may dream of natural places and fairies even after a single experience, and the joy will remain with you all the following day.

- It does not matter whether you regard what you see as objective reality filtered through your psyche, or whether the fairy essences are part of your own higher and expanded consciousness.

- The reality of such contact is in the increasing intuitive awareness and sensitivity that will benefit many aspects of your life.

CHAPTER FOUR

Fairies in Literature and Legend

The iron tongue of midnight hath told twelve;
Lovers to bed; 'tis almost fairy time.

A Midsummer Night's Dream, WILLIAM SHAKESPEARE
(1564–1616)

The oral tradition, songs, poems and tales of fairies and other magical beings was transmitted for hundreds of years in an unbroken chain by bards and minstrels after the defeat of the Druids by Julius Caesar on Anglesey (known to the Romans as Mona) in AD 43. Within these legends and verses were enshrined the hidden wisdom of the Old Religion and the tales of gods and goddesses, now disguised as mortal heroes and heroines or as fey beings of wood and hilltop. And before literacy reached the masses in the nineteenth century, ordinary people in villages and other simple settlements would recall on winter nights their grandparents' and great-grandparents' accounts of encounters with fairies, fairy gold and visits to Fairyland. These were reworked and embellished with each telling, but the core of the experience remained unchanged.

Evans-Wentz tells of *ceilidhs* in the northern isles of Scotland at which the whole community gathered, the story-teller assuming the chair of honour while outside the storms raged. In poems and songs passed from mother to child, too, the fairy legends were transmitted from generation to generation. As travellers came from distant lands, or other races conquered new countries and dedicated the old temples to their own deities, so their lore and legends mingled with the indigenous tales. Then, as people went to settle in the new colonies, the stories and songs went with them and were woven into a rich new strand of experience.

Some of the songs and stories entered the written tradition and so in a sense became more static. Many continue to be performed in folk clubs and gatherings throughout the world.

THE WRITTEN TRADITION

One of the earliest written references to fairies is in Homer's *Iliad*, in which he talks about 'watery fairies dancing in mazy rings', while in his *Odyssey* he tells of 'fair-haired dryads of the shady woods'. By medieval times, fairy lore was written down as the male children (and occasionally females) of wealthy households were educated by monks and scholars and the first universities were founded. Chaucer mentions fairies several times in his *Canterbury Tales*, most significantly perhaps in 'The Wife of Bath's Tale' in which he laments the demise of fairies under the Church.

> *In th' olde dayes of the king Artour,*
> *Of which that Bretons speken gret honour,*
> *Al was this lond fulfild of faerie;*
> *The elf-quene, with hir joly compaignie,*
> *Danced ful ofte in many a grene mede*
>
> *For now the grete charitee and prayers*
> *Of limitours and other holy freres,*
> *That serchen every lond and every streme,*
> *Blissing halles, chambres, kichenes, boures.*

Fairy Ointment

Remarkably similar accounts of a magical ointment that, if rubbed into the eyes of humans, enabled them to see fairy folk, even those wearing their cloaks of invisibility, come from all over the Celtic world.

A woman would be asked to act as a midwife to a fairy child and given magic ointment to anoint the eyes of the new-born. Often the ointment ended up being rubbed into one or both of the midwife's eyes by mistake or out of curiosity. On returning home, the woman would realise she could see fairies everywhere. Invariably she would meet and greet the fairy parent, usually the father, who would ask with which eye she saw him most clearly and then blind her in that eye.

Harsh though this seems, fairies prized their invisibility highly and any mortal who penetrated the fairy mist was regarded as a threat to their survival. Such stories suggest that fairies do share the same space as us, but operate on a different vibration.

Ballads, too, were set down in the form of poetry. Perhaps the most famous, that of Thomas the Rhymer, is still performed in folk clubs today. The real or true Thomas, as he is sometimes called, was Thomas of Earlston (Erceldoune). He was a thirteenth-century poet who met the Queen of Elfland under a magical elder tree. In return for a kiss he was forced to go to Fairyland with her, though other versions suggest Thomas was more than willing to be seduced. In a few accounts the queen becomes an ugly hag and the ritual mating of youth with the ancient Crone Goddess occurs to maintain the cycle of the seasons and ensure the fertility of the land. The version attributed to Thomas himself describes the queen:

> *Her skirt was of the grass green silk*
> *Her mantle of the velvet fine*
> *At each tett of her horse's mane*
> *Hung fifty silver bells and nine*
> *True Thomas, he pulled off his cap*
> *And bowed low down to his knee*
> *All hail, thou mighty Queen of Heaven*
> *For thy peer on earth I never did see*
> *Oh no, oh no, Thomas, she said*
> *That name does not belong to me*
> *I am but the Queen of fair Elfland*
> *That am hither come to visit thee*

Thomas remained in Elfland for seven years, though these seemed like only three days in fairy time. He was rewarded with the gifts of poetry, prophecy and a magical harp. In the ballad the fairy queen speaks of three paths: the path of thorns and briars to Heaven, the path of lily wickedness, and the 'bonnie road' to Elfland.

It has been argued in recent years that Thomas was in fact initiated into a local witch cult and that his visions of Fairyland were shamanic. Since he was already a poet, it is likely that his natural sensitivities enabled him to contact another dimension, whether through vision, dream or actuality.

AN ESCAPE FROM THE FAIRIES

But all captives were not as willing as Thomas, nor the Fairy Queen as willing to part with her mortal lover. One of the most famous tales, recorded by Robert Burns and several other poets as well as the theme of books and folk song, is that of Tam Lin, a Scottish knight who fell from his horse and was captured by the Queen of the Fairies. She bound him with magic and posted him to guard one of the entrances to the world of humans at the well of Carteraugh close to the Borders of Scotland.

Young maidens were warned not to drink at the well. Every time they did, and picked one of the roses that over-hung it, Tam Lin would appear and demand that the girl either gave him a green mantle or offered up her virginity. One bold young woman, Janet, decided to see whether the myth was true and plucked a rose from the well. She and Tam Lin fell in love, and he decided he wanted to escape from the Fairy Kingdom to marry her.

The next night was Halloween, which, Tam Lin explained, would offer an opportunity for him to escape that only occurred every seven years. The fairy ride, when the fairies moved to their winter quarters – in some versions seen as hell – would take place and the fairies would ride on horseback along the road. Tam Lin told Janet to wait for him at the crossroads near the well at midnight and to hold on to him whatever form he took.

As Tam Lin rode by in the fairy procession, Janet pulled him from his horse and held tight. Just as he had warned her, the Fairy Queen turned him into first a newt, then a snake, a tiger, a bear and finally red-hot metal. But Janet held fast and, as he became molten metal, she plunged him into the magical well.

The spell was broken. Tam Lin emerged from the water in human form and he and Janet were soon married. Shape-shifting is a feature of many ancient legends from Celtic times onwards, and is a symbol of transformation from one life form to another and so of the interconnectedness of all life.

Fairy Horses

Fairy horses were usually seen at the fairy rides or raides, adorned with bells and jewelled bridles and in perfect propor- tion to their riders – it is believed many of the miniature horse breeds are descended from these noble creatures. The horses of the king and queen had silver hooves and a crest of gold on their heads.

The most famous wild horse is the Grant Horse of English folklore who acts as a guardian to villages and warns of approaching danger. As recently as World War II, the Grant Horse is said to have warned inhabitants of the Home Counties, the Midlands, and the East Coast of air raids by driving local dogs and horses into a frenzy.

Downsizing or a Preservation of The Old Ways?

Just as the bards preserved the deities of the Old Religion in their songs and poetry, the Mother Goddess too survived in myth and secret worship as the Good Fairy, the Fairy Godmother or the Queen of the Fairies. Many of the countryside festivals and dances incorporated fairy/goddess worship into Christian practice.

The Celtic goddess Maeve, warrior Queen of Connacht, became Mab, Queen of the Fairies, also called Titania. She is the wife of Oberon, King of the Fairies, in Shakespeare's *A Midsummer Night's Dream*. In *Romeo and Juliet* Mab is called the fairy midwife and is described as far tinier than Titania, who in the *Dream* is mortal size. Juliet's nurse says to her charge:

> *Oh then, I see, queen Mab hath been with you,*
> *She is the fairy's midwife, and she comes*
> *In shape no bigger than an agate-stone*
> *On the fore-finger of an alderman*

The fairy midwife was a form of the Fate Goddesses who attended the birth of a child and determined his or her destiny (see Chapter 9).

The Horned God, consort of the Mother Goddess,

became the Fairy King Oberon (see Chapter 9), while the trickster-god role, for example Loki in the Norse tradition, was taken by the mischievous and sometimes malicious Puck of *A Midsummer Night's Dream*. In Cornish legend Puck himself was a deity, associated with the Welsh Pwca, the Black God who was appeased with offerings of fish.

A fairy in Shakespeare's play talks of Puck's mischief:

> *Are you not he*
> *That frights the maidens of the villagery,*
> *Skim milk,*
> *Mislead night-wanderers, laughing at their harm?*

The quarrel between the King and Queen of the Fairies, provoked by Puck, is seen as wreaking havoc on the land:

> *The green corn*
> *Hath rotted 'ere his youth attained a beard;*
> *The fold stands empty in the drowned field*
> *The Spring, Summer,*
> *The chiding Autumn, angry Winter,*
> *Change their wonted liveries and the mazed world*
> *By their increase, know not which is which.*

Though these are courtly fairies, the old magic is never far away and even the head of the ass fixed to the head of Bottom the workman by Puck, to play a cruel trick on Titania, is linked with ancient nature worship. It represents the wild Pan, god of unbridled nature, who comes from a tradition much earlier even than Ancient Greece.

FAIRY TALES

Out of the oral folk stories and accounts of fairies came the traditional fairy tales, although many of these were not written for children. Perrault's fairy tales, the most famous of those written down in seventeenth-century France, and those written by aristocratic women such as Madame d'Aulnoy, were intended as a commentary on court and aristocratic life. However, they were rooted in ancient folk lore. They were, like the folk stories of the German country-side collected by the Brothers Grimm in the early nineteenth century, far darker than the versions that have become familiar to children. However, the tales of neither Perrault nor Grimm cast doubt on the existence of actual fairies. Indeed, Perrault wrote: 'There is no need [for me] no need to tell you what a fairy was like in those most happy of times, for your mother has told you about them when you were very young.'

So the aristocratic fairy was born in 1697. But though Perrault's Sleeping Beauty is endowed with all the gifts she will need for a courtly life by six of the seven good fairies, even after her awakening from the curse of death administered by a forgotten eighth fairy – a hag for whom the king had no lavish gift prepared – life was far from happy ever after. The curse of the hag fairy was mitigated to a hundred years' sleep by the seventh fairy; but on awaking, the princess was left in the forest until the death of the handsome prince's father. When she was finally installed in the palace with her two forest-begotten offspring, off went the new king, her gallant husband, leaving her and her two children to be almost eaten by her ogress mother-in-law. Escaping this fate with a little magic and a lot of wit, the young queen was about to be cast into a vat filled with snakes when her husband arrived home and the ogress threw herself into the vat instead, realising she had been a little remiss in the hospitality stakes.

Of course, the really interesting characters are the hag fairy and the ogress mother-in-law, no less than the Bone Goddess of transformation (a figure that goes back to ancient history, representing the transformation of old life through rebirth); this character appears also in Perrault's story entitled *Fées* (*Fairies*). In this tale, the good but unloved maiden who gave a fairy hag a drink at the fountain was rewarded by having pearls and diamonds fall from her lips whenever she spoke. Naturally the bad daughter was sent to the fountain to seek her fortune; however, she ended up spitting vipers because she tried to trick the fairy, who this time was disguised as a princess. This motif appeared in her earthier form in the ancient Russian traditional tale of Baba Yaga, whose house was surrounded by skulls, and also in the Germanic Mother Hölle, the hag guise of the Mother Goddess, the latter told by the Brothers Grimm (see Chapter 9). What is also significant is that the true fairy stories were focused on female characters and the men were largely absent or ineffectual. It is only with Disney that the handsome prince gets the good lines; generally it is the father's absence or unwillingness to intervene that gets the beautiful young maiden cast out by the wicked stepmother, and father rarely sends out a search party.

THE MAN WHO WANTED TO LIVE IN FAIRYLAND FOR EVER

It was another woman, the author J. M. Barrie's mother, who indirectly led to the creation of *Peter Pan*. The story is of a boy who never grew up but stayed in the magical Never Never Land fighting pirates and Red Indians and aided in his endeavours by Tinkerbell the fairy. It is a children's classic, but *Peter Pan* has dark depths that echo the desperate attempts of its author to win his mother's love. When he was seven James lost his thirteen-year-old brother David in a skating accident. James's mother took to her bed and remained isolated and in mourning for years, ignoring her younger son. On one occasion when he entered her darkened room she called out, 'Oh, David, is that you? Could that be you?' before saying, 'Oh, it is only you, James.'

James became driven by a desire to imitate his dead brother so well that she would not notice the difference. Wearing his brother's clothes, Barrie would burst into his grieving mother's room and begin whistling in the special way David used to do.

But he could not replace David in his mother's affections. Worst of all, she told James many times that David had died when he was still perfect and still a boy, never to be ruined by growing up and away from his mother. Barrie's obsession with trying to please his mother would last all his life. He once said of his own old age: 'When the past comes sweeping back like the shades of night over the bare road of the present, it will not, I believe, be my youth I shall see but hers, not a boy clinging to his mother's skirts and crying, "Wait till I'm a man and you'll lie on feathers", but a little girl in a magenta frock and a white pinafore.'

The curse lay on him all his life. He did grow up physically, though as an adult he was barely 5 feet (1.5 metres) tall. His case is often mentioned in textbooks on psychogenic dwarfism, a failure to grow due to lack of maternal affection. Despite this he became one of the most popular writers in Britain in the early twentieth century, although *Peter Pan* and *The Admirable Crichton* are the only two of his works that have survived the test of time. He married a beautiful actress but was never able to consummate his marriage. Barrie's own dilemma is expounded in *Peter Pan* when Wendy tries to attract him as a woman and Peter replies: 'But Wendy, you are our mother.' Barrie was ignored by his father, and it is not by chance that in stage productions Captain Hook and Wendy's father are usually played by the same actor.

As well as the play *Peter Pan*, Barrie also wrote a book on Peter which has even more sombre undertones than the play. It follows roughly the same course as the play: Peter falls out of his pram in Kensington Gardens as a baby and is taken to Never Never Land by Tinkerbell. He returns to his home in later years to find that his mother has replaced him with another baby, having apparently forgotten him. Such was the fate of all the Lost Boys. Wendy and her brothers go to Never Never Land and after various adventures return to their home with the other Lost Boys. Peter stays in Never Never Land, although Wendy returns each year to do Peter's spring-cleaning. But Wendy grows up and marries and Peter no longer recognises her. Instead he takes her daughter to Never Never Land. The book ends with a white-haired Wendy watching her granddaughter being taken on the annual trip to Never Never Land to become Peter's mother for a brief time.

C. S. Lewis and J. R. R. Tolkien

Why should two mid-twentieth-century intellectuals and Oxford University professors create magical worlds that, certainly in the case of Tolkien with his major works *The Hobbit* and *The Lord of the Rings* trilogy, established a cult that has proved as fascinating to adults as to children.

For many decades, people worldwide have practised the Tolkien elven language and runes described in the books and re-created the world in games and in serious study of every detail of the magical lands and their inhabitants.

His novels were heavily rooted in Scandinavian folklore and their characters included elves, gnomes, goblins and, in *The Lord of the Rings*, the powerful fairy woman Galadriel, the beautiful Elf Queen. In Norse mythology the most famous ring was that created by the dwarf Andvari with cursed gold that would destroy all who wore it. These legends form the backdrop to Tolkien's cosmic dramas of good and evil, temptation and sacrifice – quests that seemed impossible but were vital to the salvation of the world by creatures called hobbits, unwillingly and unlikely heroes, with the Merlinesque wizard Gandalf, one of an order of sacred beings, as guide. The character of Gandalf, who becomes even more powerful as the White Lord after his death, first appeared in *The Poetic Edda*. The Eddas, the sacred prose and poetic sagas of the Vikings, were the earliest record of these ancient oral poems, written down by scribes from the eleventh century onwards.

Tolkien's books, especially the three that comprise *The Lord of the Rings*, tell of:

Three Rings for the Elven-kings under the sky,
Seven for the Dwarf-lords in their halls of stone,
Nine for Mortal Men doomed to die,
One for the Dark Lord on his dark throne

One Ring to rule them all, One Ring to find them,
One Ring to bring them all and in the darkness bind them

The main characters are Bilbo Baggins, hero of *The Hobbit*, and Frodo Baggins, his nephew. Hobbits are described as a race about the same height as dwarves, but much smaller, with long, nimble fingers and toes, curly hair on their heads and feet, and a liking for food that makes them quite rotund.

In *The Hobbit* Bilbo wins the Ring of the Dark Lord from Gollum, a creature originally of hobbit descent but wasted and corrupted by the ring. In *The Lord of the Rings* Sauron, the Dark Lord, has gathered to him the rings of power with which he will rule the Earth. All he needs is the Master Ring, held unwittingly by Bilbo and passed to his nephew Frodo Baggins, who is told by Gandalf that he must make the perilous journey across Middle Earth to the Cracks of Doom that lie within the territory of the Dark Lord. The only way of destroying the ring forever is by casting it into the fiery Cracks of Doom and so saving Middle Earth (see Chapter 6).

C. S. Lewis's seven Narnia books also mirrored the struggle between good and evil in a magical land peopled by dwarves, fauns and other fey creatures. Here the old goddess order was firmly on the side of evil in the person of the White Witch, whose reign meant that it was always winter and never Christmas. In the first book, *The Lion, the Witch and the Wardrobe*, the Saviour/God figure the lion Aslan, son of the Emperor across the Sea, is a willing sacrifice as the innocent victim who can save the sinner Edmund. He was one of the four children whose destiny is bound up with the fulfilment of the old prophecy that Narnia can only return to its true form when four kings and queens sit upon the four thrones at the castle of Cair Paravel.

By following a sacrifice ritual as practised in many of the ancient agrarian-based religions, Aslan rekindles the old magic from before the dawn of time and is restored to life through the reversal of time. This brings about the start of spring after the reign of the White Witch is ended. The White Witch, of course, was not really wicked at all, but merely fulfilling her role as the Hag of Winter. By Aslan's willing sacrifice to her – in the old lore the ritual mating with the young Sun God at the beginning of spring – the maiden goddess (in this case in the characters of Lucy and Susan) was brought to life and the true spring could begin. After Aslan is restored to life, he tells Lucy and Susan that 'though the witch knew the Deep magic, if she could have looked back into the stillness and darkness before Time dawned, she would have read there a different incantation'.

Lewis's books have also sparked intense philosophical interest in the significance of doors into other worlds, the entrances to Fairyland that have been identified in the everyday world as standing stones and hollow hills. At the end of the book, the Professor with whom the children were staying, tells them that they would not be able to return to Narnia via the wardrobe, as they had entered it the first time, and that they should not go looking for entrances. When the time was right for their return to Narnia, it would just happen.

Perhaps the fascination both for the scholarly authors and the readers of all ages lies in the truths expressed by the magical world that modern life can no longer satisfy spiritually. The fairy world of these books can be black and terrifying, but these realms, in which there are no real divisions between magic and spirituality, Fairyland, religion and the Otherworld, is perhaps closer to the roots of reality as understood by our distant ancestors.

EXERCISE: WRITING YOUR OWN FAIRY STORY

C. S. Lewis said of his books: 'They were not a story, just pictures. I began with a mental image of a snowy wood with a little goat-footed faun scurrying along carrying an umbrella and a pile of parcels. This picture had been in my mind since I was about sixteen. Then, one day, when I was about forty, I said to myself: "Let's try to make a story about it.'"

Jungian psychotherapists especially use myth and fairy tale to explore different aspects of the psyche. Jung believed in a Collective Unconscious, the concept of a cosmic memory bank of all past experiences, wisdom and knowledge from all ages and cultures. Some believe the Collective Unconscious can offer access to an individual's previous lives and to the future, because it operates outside linear time and space. Jung also believed this eternal memory could be accessed via the individual unconscious, in dreams, visions and universal symbols. The psychologist Bruno Bettelheim saw fairy stories as a way in which a child could experience, for example, ambivalent feelings towards a mother by projecting negativity on to the wicked witch or bad stepmother. However, they are far more than this and express truths about every person's intuitive world. So by creating your own fairy stories you can find ways through your own particular wild wood in a process akin to shamanism, whose underworld closely resembles the land of the fairy tale. Shamanism is the oldest 'green' spirituality, maintaining balance and harmony in society and the individual and connecting with the essences of fish, birds, animals, rocks and trees. This contact is made through trance states that allow the innate visionary processes of the human mind to shed insight on issues in the immediate world.

In Chapter 10 you can extend the basic structure given

here and explore specific areas, for example the Arthurian world of legend, using them as a focus for psychic development. But first create your own fairy tale.

- After dusk, light a large purple candle and burn a fragrance such as sandalwood or frankincense as oil or incense in order to enhance your psychic awareness.

- Play some gentle music, perhaps inspired by the Celtic world.

- If it is not inhibiting, use a tape recorder and speak aloud as your fantasy evolves.

- Breathe slowly, allowing the light to enclose you, and visualise a golden door in the light that you can enter.

- You are in a forest in twilight, but need not fear.

- If you look around you will see a helper animal or bird or an old wise figure who will be your guide.

- Let the story unfold, whether you are the hero/heroine, playing a supporting role or merely an observer. You may find crystal palaces, fairy princesses or elves; if you meet a dragon or wicked witch you can safely interact, knowing that it is your story and that you can write the ending.

- Try to find an entrance into Fairyland – perhaps beneath a tree, on a barge across misty water, through a hilltop or next to a standing stone.

- It may be the land of elves or wise gnomes, a fairy court, or something totally surreal and not at all like the Fairyland you thought would appear.

- Let dialogues unfold and let scenes become clear and fade as you turn over the pages of your tale.

- When you have reached a happy ending, or the end of a chapter if this is an ongoing saga, return to the forest and thence to the golden door.

- Thank your guide. Sit quietly in the candlelight and relive the images, without attempting analysis.

- When you are ready write down the story, draw, paint, create poetry, compose a song or replay your tape, and let the images form once more.

- Spend the evening in quiet contemplation and let the candle burn through naturally.

- You may dream of your fairy world and perhaps explore even further in sleep.

- After a week, try the exercise again and the story may continue or a new one may unfold.

- You may in time create your own Narnia or give pleasure to children by telling your special tales.

The insights will not necessarily offer tangible answers to your life – this is not the true purpose. Rather, the aim is to forge a connection with your own mythological heritage that for many of us comes from the combination of cultures to which our forebears belonged and above all from the collective well of wisdom.

CHAPTER FIVE
Nature Spirits

The only terms that ever satisfied me as describing Nature are the terms used in fairy books, charm, spell, enchantment. They express the arbitrariness of the fact and its mystery.

G K CHESTERTON (1874–1936)

Nature spirits are regarded by some people as essences with supernatural powers who inhabit a different dimension from our own. Unlike fairies, who have their own kingdoms, they make their homes in trees, lakes, mountains or the seas, sharing the same physical space but, as suggested in Chapter 2, on a different wavelength. To water sprites their underwater palaces are as solid as our homes on the shore and they can ride horses across the surface. Being fairies, they are able to live in our world, but, rather like astronauts on the moon, after a while they may cease to thrive.

Others would argue that nature spirits are not super-natural (above nature), but are manifestations of nature in all her forms and can be seen or heard by anyone who opens himself or herself to the natural world. Because their bodies are less dense in matter than our own, it is easy to miss them or think we are seeing a ripple on water or a face in the trees that is caused by the movement of the leaves.

As late as the twelfth century, according to Gillian Tyndall in *A Handbook of Witches*, at Wolfpits in Suffolk it was recorded that two green-coloured children who could not speak the language suddenly appeared out of nowhere. They would eat nothing but beans and were very distressed. The boy died, and it is not known what happened to the girl. Ms Tyndall believes that the old races might have lived in Britain until the end of the Middle Ages when forests were cut down and marshlands drained. However, there are still places in the world where people live close to the land, and it is likely that in the forests of the frozen north, in parts of Africa or in islands in Asia and Polynesia indigenous peoples commune with nature spirits as they always have.

COMMUNICATING WITH THE SPIRITS OF NATURE – FACT OR FALLACY?

Both Lilian and Layla in Chapter 3 felt that the essences of nature were preoccupied with their own world and did not need or welcome contact. It may be vanity on the part of the human race to assume that creatures from other dimensions are bit part players in our drama, especially if they inhabited the Earth long before mortals.

People in the industrialised world no longer see these essences so readily, perhaps for the same reason that there has been a general reduction in fairy sightings. Our modern lifestyle does not leave us time to sit and watch the world go by. Both town and country dwellers use cars rather than travelling by foot, so the wild and lonely places or the unbroken silence of a moonlit night are experienced more rarely. However, some people seek and receive communications from higher natural forces in the form of devas (see Chapter 6) who reconnect us with our natural heritage.

City farms, areas of woodland within towns, the reintroduction of indigenous species of trees, and wildlife gardens even in the centre of cities all provide homes for the natural life force in its myriad forms. Thirty years from now there may be stories of essences appearing in the jungles of foliage that are a feature of many open plan offices.

NATURE SPIRITS AND AURAS

We know that everything possesses an aura. It is the biofield that surrounds us and takes power from the life force, the Earth and the cosmos, absorbing and receiving energies from people, animals, plants and sacred places.

There are, of course, considerable variations in what is regarded as animate life. The Native North Americans and other races would argue that stones and crystals are living and so can transmit healing energies. If you have a special crystal that you use for psychic development and healing, you will be aware of the positive and powerful interactions between you and what some call the spirit of the stones.

It is likely that when our distant ancestors lived closer to the land, an awareness of auras in both nature and people was universal. Plants emit light round their forms that can be detected in Kirlian photography, a method of capturing auras on film. Plant auras fade when the plants are cut or deprived of water, and if a leaf is removed from a living plant the aura of the missing part remains, fed by the auric energies of the whole plant.

It appears that this energy is sentient and of a psychic nature. Plants respond to unspoken threats against not only themselves but others of their species. By hooking plants up to polygraph equipment (and later to electrocardiograph and electroencephalograph equipment), Cleve Backster and other researchers experimenting during the 1960s and 1970s in the USA discovered that plants not only respond to experiences in their environment but seem able to pick up on people's thoughts. The strongest readings obtained were in reaction to the destruction of living cells, whether plant, animal or human. The death of cells or even the threat of it set up intense electromagnetic reactions in the plants.

It is further projected that we all possess a spirit or etheric body, and it is the energy from this that is reflected in the varying colours of the aura. Nature spirits may be a manifestation of the etheric forms, emanating from the particular plant or tree they adopt. Indeed, because they do not need a physical form as dense as our own their aura relates to the higher, more spiritual areas of our auras; as our psychic powers are restored, so nature essences become easier to see.

ANIMALS AND FAIRIES

Fairy beings, as noted earlier, are known for shape-shifting into animals. Animals were therefore revered in the Celtic world, for if you harmed one you might be hurting a fairy. Several tribes and clans in Scotland and Ireland have taken the name of an animal, claiming descent through the legend of a fairy ancestor who adopted this form.

Deer

In the north of Scotland and the Scottish isles especially there is a long tradition of deer goddesses/fairies. These date back to the hunter tribes of the Mother Goddess who, as Mistress of the Herds, released the animals that they might be hunted for food. In northern Scandinavia, northern Canada and Siberia belief in this tradition continues.

Cailleach, the Celtic Hag Goddess, was known as the Mistress of Wild Things and took the form of a deer as one of her animal guises. Fairy women, it was said, would assume the form of a deer to escape pursuit or if enchanted by a powerful hunter magician who sought to possess them. Saba, the fairy mother of the Gaelic bard Oisin, gave birth to her son as a deer after she had been enchanted by the Dark Man of the *sidhe*, to whom she refused to give her love.

Fionn Mac Cumhal, the great leader of the Fianna, the semi-divine Celtic warriors who have been likened to King Arthur's knights, came upon Saba in her form as a white hind while he was hunting. His magical hounds, one of whom, Tyren, had herself been enchanted into dog form, would not harm the deer. Fionn took Saba home, and in the night she was transformed into a beautiful woman. She told Fionn that she could marry him and remain in human form as long as she remained within the protection of his enclosure. Saba became pregnant, but Fionn had to leave her for seven days to defend the land against the Vikings. While he was away the Dark One tricked Saba into leaving the enclosure by pretending to be the victorious Fionn returning, and he turned her once more into a white deer. Fionn hunted for seven years for his bride, without success, but at last found in a cave a golden-haired boy who told Fionn that he had been reared by his mother, a white deer. Fionn realised it was his son and named him Oisin, meaning Little Fawn. Oisin returned to his mother's fairyland when he was an adult, having fallen in love with Niamh of the Golden Hair, a fairy princess.

Fairy Cattle

These were much prized as dowries from fairy brides, especially in Wales where small, sturdy brown cattle have long thrived in mountainous conditions. The most fascinating of the fairy cow legends is that of the huge Dun Cow of Dunsmore Heath.

Originally belonging to a giant, the Dun cow provided milk to all who asked and apparently grazed happily for many years on Mitchell Fold in Shropshire. However, one day the cow became so angry when an old woman demanded that the cow filled her sieve as well as a pail with milk that she went on the rampage. She was slain by Guy, Earl of Warwick and her horns may still be seen in Warwick Castle, although some sceptics insist that they are elephant tusks.

Swans

The form of a swan was frequently adopted by fairy women and goddesses, for example the Valkyries, the beautiful Viking maidens who chose half of the noble slain to return with them to Valhalla, the Viking Heaven. In the Celtic tradition swan goddesses/fairies were famed for their wonderful voices and healing powers and were distinguishable from other swans by the gold and silver chains around their necks.

They could be forced to retain human form if a would-be lover stole their feathered cloak when they discarded it to dance by the lakeside.

The most famous of the many swan maiden tales is that of Angus Mac Og, God of Youth, son of the Irish father god, the Dagda, who lived in a palace at New Grange. One night he dreamed of a lovely fairy woman and so desired her that his mother Boanna, after whom the River Boyne is named, searched all Ireland. After more than a year the maiden was found in the form of a swan on the Lake of the Dragon's Mouth, along with 149 other swan maidens, each chained in pairs with silver and gold hung with bells. She was called Caer and was the fairy maiden of Connacht, assuming her fairy form every other year. Her father said Angus could only marry Caer if he could pick her out from the other swans. On Samhain/Halloween Angus went to the Lake of the Dragon's Mouth and instantly recognised Caer. He called her and was transformed into a swan himself. They flew away to his palace on the Boyne, creating such sweet music as they sang of their love that all who heard it slept for three days. The palace was on the site of the megalith of Brugh na Boinne, where their singing can still be heard on moonlit nights.

Because of the belief in fairy swan maidens, for many years it was forbidden to kill a swan in Ireland.

The selkie
The seal maidens or selkies of Scotland, Ireland and the North American coast were also great shape-shifters. They assumed mortal form on land and were sometimes captured

by or agreed to marry a human, but would eventually return to their own world.

A Hebridean tale recalls a fisherman of the McCodrum clan who found seven beautiful selkie sisters dancing on the shore. On the rocks near by were seven sealskins. By stealing one of the skins he was able to capture a selkie, who then lived with him in her mortal form. They had two children. But as years went on she lost her beauty, her skin flaked and she became so exhausted that she could hardly move. So she searched for her sealskin, for she knew that only by returning to the water could she survive. At last the selkie discovered her sealskin locked in a cupboard, wrapped herself in it and returned to the waves.

In some versions of the myth her only son finds the skin, restores it to his mother and dives with her into the waves, where he meets his grandfather. Though he returns to live with his father, the boy often sits on the rocks and his mother sings to him.

The clan, it is said, was thereafter called McCodrum of the Seals. Its members are said to be gifted with the second sight of the fairy people and reputed to be as much at home on the water as on land.

NATURE SPIRITS

Devas or higher natural energies are described in Chapter 6. But the tree, plant and water spirits are no less fascinating and can be very powerful, whether for good or ill. As with all fairies their power can be challenging, and sometimes flowers will be moved or a project blocked by inclement weather because a location was wrong or might have caused pollution.

Raney, a healer, therapist and poet from Camarillo in California who has studied nature spirits for many years, wrote about her experiences and those of her friend Corinne when they were creating a new garden. Some of the younger nature spirits had caused disruption to her planting: Raney believes that nature spirits will imitate human behaviour, and if they see human vandals may be tempted to act similarly. She explained:

Fairies, in truth, are very beautiful beings and never mean real harm! They are not malicious in any way, and they have a very different way of looking at life than we humans do.

Part of what they do is to copy the archetype patterns they are shown. This is how they know what shapes and colours to paint the flowers. As the human and nature kingdoms are drawing closer together, they are sometimes tempted to pattern after what we humans do, and when they see something, especially a pattern that looks like it might be fun or exciting, they will copy it. Fairies will also appear however we expect them to, shape-shifters that they are. If we expect to see them as Victorian-looking, they will, or as the colour of the flowers that they are assigned to paint, they will show us that. Sometimes they flit around as tiny points of light which is especially beautiful to see.

Both Corinne and I have been seeing fairies in the corner of our eyes a lot lately, as well as the gnomes and other nature beings. Every now and then one of them would dart past, or into a bush or rock. We were amazed and very pleased that they were showing themselves to us and wanted more contact. We also knew that the fairies, especially, were very tricky and playful. But we never expected this.

The more we thought about it and the more we looked around, the more evidence we found of their mischievous activities. They were having the time of their life!

But they were also giving us a message. I had been talking a lot with the gnomes, the devas and all the other wee folk, so I think the fairies felt neglected.

While planting the Scottish and Irish moss I had a lot of conversations with my friends, the Leprechauns, and with the gnomes. They have helped so much with this magical garden and are always around.

Picturing nature spirits

Some people have attributed human form to these essences, as Raney points out – and so we may see them in this way. The artist Cicely Mary Barker is well known for capturing the essence of plant, flower and tree fairies, many of whom are far from saccharine sweet. She was born in 1895 in Croydon near London and because of childhood illness spent most of her life at home, where she passed many hours in the garden. In this way she acquired the stillness that seems necessary to observe essences within nature, as one might a shy rare bird or butterfly.

Cicely began to paint her images shortly after the story of the Cottingley Fairies had aroused a desire among adults for a return to innocence and beauty. The fairies she depicted were based on her intimate knowledge of the essential qualities within different plants and flowers and her artistic studies of real children, each dressed to represent the spirit of a different flower or tree. The success of her first book in 1923, in which she also wrote verses about the fairies, led to seven more. She continued to paint until her eyesight began to fail towards the end of her life, and died in 1973 at the age of seventy-seven. Recently her fairies have been made into figurines that are proving popular on both sides of the Atlantic.

Magical Trees

Wherever the three magical trees oak, ash and thorn grow together is a place where fairies gather, and the space between two oaks offers an entrance to Fairyland.

Willows, sacred to the Moon Goddess and the Crone Goddesses are said to move at night. The elder is the ultimate fairy tree and if you wear a crown of elder twigs on May Eve (30 April) you will be able to see these magical creatures.

You may see fairies if you sit beneath a hawthorn at twilight. But don't shelter under one on May Eve, Midsummer Eve or Halloween, or you will become enchanted by the fairies. Single thorns growing near fairy hills and those in threes are especially magical.

Some trees and plants act as a deterrent to malevolent fairies and witches. Rowan was regarded as protective against enchantment. Rowan crosses uncut by metal were tied with red twine and placed on barns and outhouses on May morning to keep away bad fairies, while a rowan twig was tied to a cow's tail to stop fairies stealing the milk. Rowan cradles were carved to protect babies from being stolen by the fairies. A wreath of mistletoe did the same job.

The spirits of trees

Tree spirits are found in many cultures. In Africa, they are still held in high regard as tribal gods and benign spirits who control sunshine and rain and the fertility of crops and women.

Japanese mythology is rich in tree deities and spirits. Uku-No-Chi was the deity who lived in tree trunks and Hamori protected the leaves of trees. Each tree was under the guardianship of a god. In more popular myth wood spirits were depicted in human form but with the heads and claws of hawks.

Dryads are female tree spirits, of whom the hamadryads are one kind. They are described in Ancient Greek literature and are also found in Celtic mythology in the traditions of places to which people of Celtic ancestry emigrated. Many live in willows, trees sacred to the Moon Goddess whose creatures they are, since they emerge into the woodland mainly at night when their beautiful singing can be heard, especially when it is windy. Dryads also care for other sacred trees, notably oak, ash and thorn.

The Ghillie Dhu are Scottish tree spirits who live mainly in birch trees and hide in foliage to avoid observation. Less benign than dryads, they would sometimes bind travellers fast with fronds and transport them to Fairyland.

Tree elves, found in Norway as well as Scotland, have

been described as quite tiny and dressed in green and are expert herbalists for woodland animals as well as for their own kind. However, they do not share their knowledge with humans.

Hyldermoder or Elder Mothers are Scandinavian and northern European tree fairies that live in elder trees, the most magical of all fairy plants, and are linked with the ancient Mother Goddess. Not until medieval times were these fairies demonised as wicked witches. The legend of the Rollright Stones, ancient standing stones in Oxfordshire, concerns a hag goddess/fairy who guarded the countryside. The stones were an invading king and his army whom she turned to stone. She then transformed herself into an elder tree close to the stones to stand sentinel in case the enchantment was broken. On Midsummer Eve, locals would go to the King-stone and after a feast would ceremonially cut the elder tree, which then bled to bring fertility to the land.

In 1962 a young boy assisting a local farmer was driving a tractor on a hill above the nearby village of Long Compton at about 10 p.m. on a summer night. He suddenly saw a 'white pillar' of hazy light, about 15 feet (5 metres) in front of the tractor, that hovered in the air for a few seconds before gradually disappearing.

When I visited the stones in the spring of 2000, hoping to find the Elder Mother, I was told the tree had been cut down because of vandalism, though it had apparently been a focus for ribbon tying, a custom performed in celebration of the spirit of the tree, and other offerings. However, there are bushes of elder near the King-stone, so I hope the old lady will rise again.

A similar female mother tree figure, though more glamorous (except when she shape-shifts into a hag), is the Swedish wood nymph, Huldra or Skogsra, described as a beautiful woman living deep in the forest where she is the caretaker of the woods and wild animals. Even today in remote regions hunters leave her tributes and ask her permission to hunt. Huldra is a form of Frigga, the Viking Mother Goddess.

UNDERGROUND SPIRITS

Mine spirits

The most famous mine spirits are the knockers of Cornwall. However, mine spirits exist in lands from South America to eastern Europe – wherever people work underground. Because it is a dangerous occupation, taking place in semi-darkness, aspects of the other world are close even to the most cynical miners; so the protection of the mine spirits is invoked, though but no means certain. The true owners of the mines are the spirits. Indeed, it was said that greedy mine owners who respected neither the spirits nor the workers caused the spirits to withdraw their bounty, for example in the tin, gold and copper mines of Cornwall – though it was the miners themselves who suffered most by their closure.

Dwarf-like and only occasionally seen, the Cornish knockers directed the miners to rich seams of mineral ore or coal. Though they did display the unpredictability of nature spirits and sometimes set up knocking noises to confuse the workers, the knockers acted as guardians, rapping frantically if there was danger. Legends tell how mine spirits have guided rescuers to trapped miners. Mine spirits hate whistling, and so this is considered unlucky while underground.

Our Lady of the Mineshaft

In South America the Pachamama is the female consort of the male fertility or thunder deity. Since the introduction of Catholicism the benign aspects of the Pachamama have become associated with the Virgin Mary, who has taken over several of her former shrines. For example, in the tin mines of Bolivia the earth deities are appeased with offerings each day, and the miners invoke the protection of the Virgin Mary or Our Lady of the Mineshaft against the male and female earth demons, the old pagan deities who have taken on hostile aspects.

WATER FAIRIES

Lake spirits

Lake spirits are generally beautiful long-haired women who live in palaces beneath the water and come ashore to dance and seek human husbands with whom to procreate. There may be a male King who emerges to negotiate the lake maiden's dowry, but male lake spirits are rarely recorded.

Gwragedd Annwn are beautiful Welsh fair-haired fairy women, the same size as humans, living in underwater palaces in lakes close to the Black Mountains. These lake maidens have on occasions taken human husbands, though they rarely stayed with them. Some local families still claim fey heritage.

The Lady of the Lake in Llyn y Fan Fach is the fairy ancestor of an unbroken line of Welsh healers and physicians, and, unusually, this fairy legend can be dated. Records from around 1230 tell that a young farmer saw three beautiful women dancing on the shore; the most beautiful agreed to be his wife and her father, the King of Faery, came from under the lake to bestow a dowry of fairy cattle. However, he imposed a number of conditions on her staying that vary according to the teller, for at this point the facts become clouded with fairy dust. One condition was that she should never be touched with iron, another that she should not be made to go to church, and yet another that if her husband struck her three times she and her dowry would return to the lake.

The couple had three sons, but the farmer broke his bargain – though, according to male tellers of this tale, the poor husband only tapped the fairy lightly and for good reason. But a fairy bargain being a fairy bargain, off went cattle and fair maiden. However, she did come back to teach her sons knowledge of herbs and healing; they became the Physicians of Myddfai, healers to the Welsh kings. When they died they left a medical treatise, copies of which exist today.

Well spirits

These go back to time immemorial at sacred wells and springs. However, they are usually invoked under the name of a Christian saint who replaced the original otherworldly guardian of the well or spring.

Well spirits are shape-shifters, being witnessed most commonly as beautiful women in white such as the Breton Corrigans who are seen close to wells, fountains and sacred springs. In Brittany also are *les bonnes dames*, the elderly gossips in traditional high lace hats who congregate around the village fountain at night, as the earthly dowagers do in the daytime.

Well spirits are traditionally invoked for female fertility, and until the late nineteenth century some wells, especially in Scotland and Ireland, retained a female mortal guardian. This was usually an old woman who instructed suppliants in the old rituals. The interest in fertility wells and their guardians is currently undergoing a great revival. Sacred wells, representative of the entrance to the womb of the Earth Mother, have always been a source of power for healing and divination as well as fertility.

Pilgrims to the Celtic capped well, known as the Well of the Triple Goddess at Minster Abbey Gatehouse on the Isle of Sheppey in Kent, have over the past few years reported seeing a lady dressed all in white who disappears when approached. 'Like a bride on her wedding day' is how she was described by one observer. Christians interpret the presence as a vision of the Virgin Mary, while others call her simply the White Lady. A strong scent of flowers or perfume is also reported by pilgrims as they push coins as votive offerings between the paving cracks of the Minster well.

Even as late as the nineteenth century country girls would visit holy wells in order to dream of a future husband. One such divinatory place was the Fairy's Pin Well, in Selby in Yorkshire, so named after the custom of young women to drop bent pins – made of gold or silver if the suppliant was wealthy – as offerings. In one recorded case, a servant girl visited the well and, having made her wish, fell asleep by the well. One of her suitors, dressed in wedding finery, then brought her a wedding ring and took her to Elf-land for feasting and revelry.

SPIRITS OF THE SEA

Merpeople are invariably regarded as beautiful women, with human heads and bodies to the waist but a fish tail below the waist. Though they are dismissed by sceptics as seals or other sea creatures, for centuries sailors have brought back tales of beautiful sea women with lovely voices appearing in all parts of the world. Usually merpeople are helpful, saving drowning sailors and guiding ships away from rocks, though occasionally they can be malevolent; they are seen in shoals around islands that have magical associations.

Mermaids, like selkies, have married mortal men. This usually occurs through trickery when the human steals one of their possessions and so binds them to dry land. However, there have been love matches, as in Hans Andersen's *Little Mermaid*. At the age of fifteen, on her first visit to the surface of the water, the mermaid saves the life of a prince in a shipwreck and falls in love with him. She goes to a sea witch who promises her legs and says that, if the prince loves her more than any other, the mermaid will gain a soul. But to become human, the price is very high. In return the mermaid has to give the witch her lovely voice, and every step she takes on land is like walking on red-hot needles.

In spite of her sacrifice, the prince marries a princess. The mermaid cannot return to the sea except as foam, unless she kills the prince before his marriage. This she refuses to do, and plunges into the sea. However, since this is a fairy tale, albeit a fairly dark one, her goodness is rewarded and she is taken up by the sylphs, the archetypal air spirits, and so gains the chance of earning a soul by good deeds.

DARKER WATER SPIRITS

Not all water spirits are benign, and Chapter 9 describes the Morgana, the terrifying though lovely sea women who drag their lovers to a watery grave. In the same way, the original Lorelei was a beautiful young female fairy who sat on the cliffs above the River Rhine and, like the Sirens of Greek myth, sang haunting songs that were said to be irresistible, so luring sailors to their deaths on the rocks below. The term 'Lorelei' is now a generic one for female water spirits in Europe, specially those of fresh water.

Nereids are the Greek water maidens of the Classics, associated especially with the Aegean Sea, but are found from Scandinavia to Crete. A negative connotation of ocean power, the nereids are said to drive mad anyone who perceives them under a full moon. Because they cannot bear children, they are believed to kidnap human ones. They can venture on land wearing a white shawl, which if stolen gives the mortal who takes it power over them. They also shape-shift as swans, in which form their lovely but hypnotic voices may be heard. They are also claimed as kin by families in the Greek islands.

EXERCISE: AN EMPOWERING MOON AND TREE RITUAL

● Find a fairy tree – a hawthorn, elder, ash, willow or oak – and sit beneath its branches on a bright moonlit night during the week of the full moon so you can see the moon through the branches. Look upwards and feel the positive energies of the cosmos flowing into you.

● Watch the moonlight filter through the leaves and make patterns, and you may be aware of living, moving energies within the branches and leaves.

- Touch the trunk with your hands and let the life force of the tree flow into you, so that you can feel the pulsating energies of its essence, like mild electricity.

- Standing, and still touching the tree, press your feet down towards the roots, letting all negativity, anxiety or exhaustion flow from you into the ground. Press really hard.

- Now raise your arms to make contact with the moon-dappled leaves and draw strength and healing from them.

- Move away from the tree and, keeping the moon in view, go round the tree nine times clockwise in ever-decreasing circles, letting your feet guide you. The nine circles of power are an ancient magical device. If you now stand within the innermost ring, reaching out to the trunk with just your fingertips, you may momentarily make contact with the spirit of the tree.

- Spend a little longer watching the moonlight filter through the leaves and amplifying the tree energies, and make a wish upon the moon.

CHAPTER SIX

Devas and Elementals

We are the voices of the wandering wind,
Which moan for rest and rest can never find;
Lo! as the wind is, so is mortal life,
A moan, a sigh, a sob, a storm, a strife.

'The Deva's Song', SIR EDWIN ARNOLD
(1832–1904)

The term *deva* in the ancient Eastern language Sanskrit means 'shining one'. Devas or adhibautas represent the higher forms of nature essences, akin to angels, the opalescent beings who watch and direct the natural world. They communicate with people either through channelling or psychic communication, or directly through the healing and restorative properties of herbs, flowers and trees.

The current view of devas has evolved from Hinduism and Buddhism. These entities are far more abstract and so less readily described than the shining beings of the old Gods of Dana (the Celtic gods and goddesses) whose fairy court rivalled the finest in Europe. It was Madame Helena Blavatsky, founder of the Theosophical Society, who brought the concept of devas as angelic beings to the West. She believed that, when humanity had achieved a high enough state of spiritual evolution, devas would enter into communication with mortals to help them to develop further. Since devic communication is now apparently occurring, it may be that humans are ready to accept this higher form of wisdom – though it may also be that the dire state of the planet has perhaps accelerated the need for higher forms of nature to intervene. Though devas do primarily relate to the natural world, they transmit messages concerning the need for peace and harmony, as well as caring for all of nature's creatures.

COMMUNICATING WITH DEVAS

In the Native North American culture, more highly evolved essences were manifest as the King of the Beavers or Lord of the Eagles. This being might offer special strength or wisdom to those alone in a forest or on a mountain, whether on an initiatory or a personal spiritual Vision Quest. Vision Quests were undertaken by Native Americans as part of their initiation into adulthood and at other spiritually significant times. They involved going out into the wilderness, fasting and meditating until inspiration came, usually in the form of visions. It is a method adopted, usually under less rigorous conditions, by people who wish to reconnect with the natural world and their inner selves.

Devas are said to be aware of the thoughts of humans and can channel messages to those who are sufficiently sensitive to hear them, using clairaudient (heard within the mind) and telepathic means, especially when a person is in a state of meditation close to the natural world. Channelling is a way of receiving messages of wisdom, usually clairaudiently, that are attributed to a higher spiritual source, whether an angel, a spirit guide, a spiritual essence of the more evolved part of the self. Some cynics say that city folk have their angels and country dwellers have their devas. There is indeed an overlap between devas and those angels who communicate with humans (see below). Described frequently as appearing in the form of beautiful humans, though they inhabit the etheric or astral plane (the realm of the spirit body), devas can change size and appearance almost instantly, perhaps to harmonise with the image system of the perceiver.

DEVIC POWER

Devas are credited with great powers in the skies, water and earth, exploding star clusters, regulating the tides and creating perfume in flowers.

In eastern philosophy it is said that trees can provide a home for devas who do not assume a permanent form. This may be the origin of the oracular or sacred trees that are found in different cultures and ages. For example, the prophetic oak sacred to the Greek Father God Zeus stood in the oracular groves at Dodona. A piece of the tree was placed in the *Argo*, the boat of Jason and the Argonauts, to give them guidance on their quest for the Golden Fleece.

Other devas assume the role of sacred guardian at ancient sites and have been described as huge brown shadows as dusk draws in, or as silver columns of light when dawn breaks through. Devas communicate telepathically with humans, and devic communication can occur quite spontaneously in a beautiful garden or woodland. It can also be induced using meditation or by visualising a deva and allowing words to form. In the Icelandic and Scandinavian traditions that spread to other parts of northern Europe, including Britain, the land wights or *landvaeitir* acted as guardians of villages and settlements, passing along the fairy paths at dusk and enclosing the area in their protection. Certain fields and hills were declared sacred to them and could not be built on or even ploughed.

Devas are also associated with one of the four elements of Earth, Air, Fire and Water and rule over the Elemental beings (see p. 130). In Wicca and ceremonial magic devas are called Lords of the Watchtower and represent the Four Quarters of the Ritual Circle. Sometimes Archangels take on this role: for instance Michael, Archangel of the Sun, is linked with Fire and Gabriel, the Archangel of the Moon, with Water.

THE DEVAS OF FINDHORN

At Findhorn in Morayshire in north-east Scotland, a beautiful garden has been created on barren soil and the place has evolved into a centre of world spirituality. Peter Caddy, a former senior officer in the Royal Air Force, his wife Eileen, their three sons and Dorothy, a colleague, created the garden in 1962 with the help of devas who instructed Peter on the planting and care of the vegetables and flowers. Vegetables far larger than normal grew in soil where previously even weeds had not survived. A 40 lb (18 kg) cabbage was seen growing in sand by newspaper reporters. The devas communicated the message that the garden was an example of how harmony and growth of spirit could be achieved within the wider world.

DEVAS AND HEALING

Devas have also been associated with the discovery and creation of flower and tree essences. In the case of the Findhorn Flower Essences, different flower devas guided the creator to those flowers that had the necessary healing qualities to produce a comprehensive range. Marion Leigh, who came from Australia to Findhorn, described the process: 'I had no overall plan to include any particular flowers in the range, so that the flowers found me. The exception to this was the Scottish primrose, a rare plant: the message that came through [from this flower] was so powerful: the gift I bring is peace. Just one drop of my essence has the power to infuse the hearts of the masses, so treat me with great respect and I will manifest peace in God's graceful timing.'

Magical Flowers

Many of the prohibitions against picking fairy flowers are environmentally sound and ensured the survival of certain species in the wild for centuries.

The blue flowers of bluebells ring to call fairies to their revels at midnight and on the fairy festivals. Therefore the flowers should not be picked or bad luck will follow. With their clusters of small yellow flowers on each stamen, cowslips are said to reveal fairy gold buried nearby. They are protected by the fairies and it is considered unlucky to remove them from their natural habitat.

Elves and pixies shelter in ferns, so it is important not to crush them or speak close to them of secrets that may be carried to the four winds. In Russia it is said that, when ferns bloom golden at Midsummer, a handful of the seeds should be cast in the air. Where they fall will reveal hidden gold.

Foxgloves are the ultimate fairy flower. The purple or white cups were worn as hats and the whole flower provided shelter for tiny fairies. When a foxglove bows its head, it is a sign that a fairy is passing by. Foxgloves are considered very lucky if grown in a garden from seed, but they must never be transplanted since they may well be home for a fairy. Note that they are poisonous.

In Irish tradition, lilies of the valley form ladders that fairies can climb to reach the reeds from which they plait their cradles. These flowers are poisonous.

Primroses may be yellow, white, pink or purple and are sacred both to the Mother Goddess and to the Druids. A bunch of five freshly gathered primroses, especially if growing near water, is said to open the way to Fairyland if placed on a magical standing stone.

St John's wort, the yellow herb of Midsummer has divinatory powers. If gathered at dusk by young maidens who have fasted all day and placed beneath their pillows, the herb promises dreams of true love. However, stepping on St John's wort may cause a fairy horse to rise up and take the mortal on a wild ride lasting all night.

Thistledown transports fairies, as do dandelion clocks, and in return for sending a fairy on its way you may have a wish. This may not be popular near cultivated gardens!

The Australian Native Tree Essences were developed by Judi Harvey in 1992, but her inspiration began in childhood. She grew up in northern New South Wales, in a subtropical rain forest used by Aboriginal peoples for at least four thousand years. Her knowledge was developed while studying at the Flower Essence Centre in Melbourne, but, as with all flower and tree essences, the discovery of their powers is frequently a process rooted in spirituality and magic, actively inspired by interaction with the nature spirits.

Judi wrote:

Each of the thirteen trees appeared to me [in devic form] with positive and adverse healing properties. Each tree has natural associations with a colour and I started to receive these insights through my meditations and intuitions. At the new moon I was told to collect new and old leaves, twigs and barks, put them in Australian spring water in a diamond-cut, diamond-shaped crystal bowl and leave it under our avocado tree during the new moon. Then I was to do a hand dance to invoke the appropriate spiritual hierarchy and nature spirits to help co-create and co-manufacture each new essence. At the full moon, I was to collect the new bud, the flower, the seedpod and the seed. This went on for thirteen lunar moon cycles, a complete lunar year.

The Australian Native Tree Essences work on the mind and spirit, and better health follows as the user is reconnected with the life force. As Judi comments: 'The Essences raise our consciousness to the level of the plants, birds, minerals and devas to make us aware of our connection and inter-dependence with nature. These essences reconnect us to the universe and especially to the rhythms of the moon.'

As well as being used as a tool for healing the self and others, these essences can be used as a focus for healing the planet.

ELEMENTALS

Rather than being creatures with a permanent form, the elementals are the forces or energies that in nature and magic give shape to living things and bring thoughts and desires into actuality, for example seeds into flowers and trees. The power of Fire, kindled symbolically in a candle flame, will burn away a piece of paper containing words or an image of what is no longer needed (see p. 136).

Elementals are believed to have the power to change their size and appearance almost at will. They take on a particular form for a particular task, and there are pictures in sixteenth-century alchemical tracts, of stick-like elemental beings, in the case of a Fire elemental resembling a flickering flame. Indeed, it is said they can hold a particularly potent form for a thousand years, before being reabsorbed into the source element.

Elementals have been associated for hundreds of years with more formal magical traditions, precisely because they are believed to transform into actuality thought forms invoked by symbols. Thus medieval occultists sought mastery over the elemental beings that they fashioned by their incantations. Sometimes, if magicians used the elemental forces for negative purposes, they would create a tulpa or thought form that became an elemental demon. This entity was hard to banish, even though magicians worked within a square enclosed by two magic circles; in extreme cases the tulpa might destroy its creator – hence the warnings about magical effects coming back threefold.

It could be argued that the ring possessed by the hobbit Bilbo Baggins in Tolkien's *Lord of the Rings* (see Chapter 4) was an elemental thought, being forged from fire by Sauron the Dark and therefore contained within the metal. The power of the ring grew by feeding on the emotions of the wearer, and it attempted to destroy all who wore it. Only when Frodo Baggins threw the ring into the fire in the

Cracks of Doom was the elemental demon reabsorbed by its source. The ring was created for a dark purpose, and so the elemental fed on the original dark power.

But equally an elemental might be created, perhaps by a deva, for an entirely positive purpose. Taking the example of the forest, an elemental being would give the energy and structure for a seed to grow into its own species which would then be inhabited by a tree spirit. The deva would guard the whole forest and coordinate the growth/decay/ new life cycle, striving to maintain the healing, life-giving force being damaged by deforestation.

On an everyday level, if emotions are running sufficiently high, elementals can link into human feelings and amplify them, at the extreme causing poltergeist activity if people are angry or enervated over a long period. Because elemental fire can be manifest as anger, it is important only to invoke magical energies when you are calm and for a positive purpose to avoid generating less benign powers. It is unlikely you will release a demon if you are fuming over an injustice as you work, but you may end up with a headache or insomnia.

THE FOUR ELEMENTS AND ELEMENTAL BEINGS

Elementals were first categorised by the Greek Neo-Platonists (a group of philosophers who combined the theories of Plato with Eastern mysticism), around the third century AD, though they were recognised much earlier as being present in Earth, Air, Fire and Water, preceding mortals. They are believed to have been the children of Lilith, reputed to have been Adam's first wife, who was cast out for refusing to submit to him.

Indeed Plato, the Greek philosopher who lived around 360 BC, recounted in his book *Timaeus* that Demiurge, the creator god, made the world out of the four elements. This world included the Earth and the celestial sphere of moon, stars and sun.

This is not entirely fanciful. If one accepts that the universe began from a core source of energy as the undifferentiated Godhead, the four elements can be regarded as one of the focused energy sources that for centuries were believed to be the building blocks of life. This included people, a concept that was used by the psychologist Jung in his Earth/sensations, Air/thought, Fire/intuition and Water/feelings categories of human functioning.

The elemental beings, as manifestations of these forces, are believed to occupy a kingdom between the material and spiritual plane and so act as a bridge between the two dimensions. The Theosophists, who introduced eastern philosophical ideas into western magical traditions in the latter part of the nineteenth century, placed them between the devas and the nature spirits in the hierarchy of spiritual beings.

The sixteenth-century alchemist Paracelcus, who is credited with great medical and magical expertise, identified personified forms of the elemental forces: the gnomes of the Earth, who may also be manifest as rock sculptures; the salamanders or legendary Fire elementals; the sylphs of the Air; and the undines of the Water. This is quite a complex idea, because a gnome itself is a fairy being. So how can he be an elemental force, and why choose a gnome and not a dwarf? The categories were merely a way of choosing an example that seemed specially to symbolise the force. But of course, if you or I had been a sixteenth-century alchemist, we might have picked a dwarf or a mermaid instead of an undine.

Some magicians have six categories of elementals, identifying fauns or satyrs as the archetypal elemental spirits of animal life and dryads, described in Chapter 5, as the core spirits of vegetation. They are also experienced as forces of nature, lightning, a raging torrent, a landslide, high winds, any dramatic movement caused by natural phenomena, and in gentler form as flickering fire fairies, winged butterflies or ancient stones seen through mist, dancing water maidens captured momentarily in a surge of foam, or as sunlight making rainbows in the centre of a waterfall. And though any self-respecting wizard would have me drummed out of the Magic Circle for saying so, you can visualise these formless powers in any way you like, as long as it is positive, and use them to enhance your inner elemental strengths.

For whether in magic or personally, the elemental essences can draw out the best qualities inherent in that element – the wisdom and persistence of Earth, the quicksilver communicative and logical abilities of Air, the inspiration and illumination of Fire, and the adaptability and empathy of Water – to help bring to fruition any wishes in the actual world.

Gnomes

The archetypal elemental spirits of the Earth, gnomes, originate in northern Europe. These ancient dwarf-like creatures are said to live mainly underground or in deep forests for a thousand years.

They are ruled by Gob, whose throne is covered with crystals, silver and gold. He is the guardian of miners and others who work within the Earth, and of those fairies who live or work in the Earth, for example dwarves and knockers, the Cornish mine fairies, leprechauns and tree spirits. In some Wiccan traditions the ruler of the gnomes is called Boreas, whose name is that of the Roman God of the North Wind.

Earth elementals are invoked in magic through ritual objects associated with the Earth element, such as the bell, pentacle and cauldron or ritual dish, and through crystals, herbs, salt and bread. They provide a focus for spells for protection, for animals, in herb magic and for property, fertility and prosperity.

On a personal and less formal level, the benign power of earth elementals can be invoked through crystals, especially those with inclusions (fossilised insects or plants within the crystals) such as amber or rutilated quartz, moss agate and jade. Earth elementals are sometimes focused in a more female way with Galadriel, Queen of the Earth Fairies, made famous in Tolkien's *Lord of the Rings* (see Chapter 4), the original Fairy Godmother, who is especially potent in natural settings such as woodlands.

Sylphs

These winged Air spirits live for hundreds of years and can, it is said, attain an immortal soul through good deeds. They never seem to age and are said to reside on mountain tops. Their ruler, Paralda, lives on the highest mountain of Earth. Sylphs may assume human form for short periods of time, and vary in size from very small up to human stature, but are most usually seen in the wind.

Magically, the Air elementals may be represented by the athame or ritual knife, by the sword or by incense. They are invoked in rituals where there is a need for logic, learning or clear communication, or for travel and career. On a personal level they can be invoked by incense or by burning aromatic oils.

Salamanders

These are the elemental spirits of Fire, the legendary fire lizard which originated in the deserts of the Middle East. They are the most powerful of the elementals and the least related to humans, though they have been perceived as small balls of light (see Chapter 7). Their ruler is a flaming being called Djin.

Described as fire lizards about a foot or more in length, or as elongated wand-like beings in the shape of flames, sala-manders live in volcanoes or lakes of fire. They can also be seen in forest fires – the larger the source of fire, the greater the perceived size of the fairy. Like the chameleon, they are constantly changing and moving, like flame itself.

Magically they may be represented by a wand, candle

flame or sacred fire and can be invoked to bring power, light, inspiration, creativity, energy and cleansing. On a personal level they can be invoked through a candle flame.

Undines

These elemental spirits of Water who originated in the Aegean Sea live in coral caves under the ocean, on the shores of lakes, on the banks of rivers or in marshland. They shimmer with all the colours of water in sunlight and are so insubstantial that they can rarely be seen, except clairvoyantly or as a rainbow within a waterfall or fountain. The ruler of the undines is a being called Necksa.

In magical tradition, the Water elementals are associated with the chalice or ritual cup and with water itself or wine. They are invoked for love and sex magic, for healing, relationship issues and children. On a personal level they can be contacted on the seashore, by rivers or through scrying in water ('perceiving dimly' is the literal meaning of the word and refers to gazing into any reflective surface to see, with the external or clairvoyant eye, images that symbolise relevant factors in the questioner's life), either by moonlight or by dropping ink or candle wax on to the surface to create moving images.

EXERCISE: COMMUNICATING WITH DEVAS

When we try to channel information, it can be difficult to distinguish between what comes from within our own psyche and what emanates from a higher source of consciousness. In a sense it does not matter, because there are no real divisions between inspiration from our own higher levels of consciousness and that from angelic or devic sources. So you may feel more comfortable thinking of your channelling as inspired by the deva within.

- Visit a botanical garden or another place with beautiful well-tended gardens that have been created by people with a love of flowers.

- Choose a clear day and walk around the garden until you find a large array of flowers that feel right for you. Fragrant flowers are especially evocative.

- Sit comfortably on a seat or rug on the grass so that you are almost surrounded by the colour.

- Relax by visualising a butterfly settling first on your head. Deliberately hold your head still, and then when it flutters on to the next part of your body relax your head and face and concentrate on remaining quite motionless for the butterfly.

- When the butterfly has finally settled on both feet and eventually flown away, you should be quite relaxed.

- Inhale gently through your nose the colour and fragrance of the flowers, letting it suffuse your whole being, and breathe out through your mouth darkness and stagnation.

- Don't worry about counting breaths, but as you concentrate on the colour a rhythm will gradually establish itself.

- As you breathe, allow the flowers to merge in your mind's vision and see or visualise a face forming within the flowers. It may be old, beautiful, beyond conventional beauty, or perhaps brown and wrinkled like a being who lives close to the soil.

- You may, however, see a mist of a paler shade forming, a patch of brilliance or pure white light.

- Any or all of these may be perceived with your inner or external eye.

- You may hear either within your head or externally a disembodied voice, or the communication may be filtered through your own voice and thoughts.

- Don't ask any questions, but wait. You may hear a line of poetry, a phrase or story, or see images. The communication may be complex or, like many profound experiences, remarkably simple. There may be a sense of peace, warmth and of being loved, rather than words or pictures.

- All these are equally valuable, and for every person who receives a volume of philosophy a hundred others will receive more subtle but equally meaningful communication.

- You may feel a sudden breeze or chill or hear someone approaching. This is time to close the channels.

- Let the face fade, and as it does so draw the colour of the flowers as a sphere to protect you and enclose you.

- Silently thank the deva and visualise a flower all around you, enfolding you in its petals as your psychic energies close.

- Walk quietly around the gardens, feeling any excess energy flowing through your feet into the earth.

- Go to a café or straight home and in your diary journal note down any words or images you recall. Don't force them — the experience was important for its own sake.

- If possible, buy a few similiar flowers to plant in your garden or window box.

- Experiment with different flowers, herbs and trees to allow the wisdom to unfold. Continue, where practical, to create your inspiring devic garden or window box to keep a little of the magic with you.

CHAPTER SEVEN

Fairies and Earth Energies

Fairy places, fairy things,
Fairy woods where the wild bee wings,
Tiny trees for tiny dames —
These must all be fairy names!

'The Flowers', ROBERT LOUIS STEVENSON
(1850–1894)

There are many ancient hilltop earth forts throughout the Celtic world that are called fairy forts and regarded as entrances to Fairyland. In the Cotswold hills in England there are more than seventy fairy hills that are hollow, some dating from 2000 BC.

By no means all of these fairy hills were used as burial chambers, though from early times offerings were left near hollow hills because they were regarded as natural places of power. This is one practice that has continued. When I visited the burial chamber at West Kennet Longbarrow, on one of the major leys that radiate from nearby Avebury and Silbury Hill in Wiltshire, I found offerings of coins, crystals and flowers that had been left both on the mound above and within the chamber, in which a scented votive candle was burning. Indeed, a fifteenth-century spell for summoning fairies suggests burying hazel wands beneath one of these fairy forts.

The hilltop forts are joined by fairy paths, the ancient ley lines, tracks of psychic energies, hypothesised by Alfred Watkins, a Herefordshire miller and naturalist, to have been prehistoric trading routes. In 1925 Watkins's book *The Old Straight Track* was published, but it was not until 1936 that the first psychic associations with these tracks as lines of energy were made when Dion Fortune published her novel *The Goat-Foot God* (still in print).

FAIRIES AND LEY LINES

It has been well attested that ghost sightings abound along lines of energy, but legends of fairies and other magical beings also exist on or close to the lines. Such places frequently bear names associated with fairies, which suggests that the tales had a basis in actual sightings. For example, on the Isle of Wight where I live Puckaster Cove is on the southernmost tip of the north–south Rue Street ley line. Puck, the trickster fairy, also called Robin Goodfellow, is associated with Jack o' the Green and the Green Man, the God of Vegetation of the old fertility legends (see p. 147).

Puckaster Cove is a place where the fairies held their revels at the full moon and on Walpurgisnacht (May Eve). They kept their gold in puffballs but guarded it jealously from mortals. One May Eve in full moonlight, the story goes, a man returning from a wedding was walking along the shore when he saw a strange golden light that led him to the cove, where he came upon the fairy feast. The man was made welcome by the fairies, who offered him food and drink that he had never tasted before, danced for him in the moonlight to the music of their pipes and sent him on his way with gold from their puffballs, saying he should never be poor again. The man became a wealthy landowner, and many have followed his path to Puckaster Cove on moonlight nights to pick the puffballs that shine golden under the moon. But by morning they have crumbled to dust.

Another Isle of Wight fairy legend focuses on the main east–west ley at Godshill that eventually joins the mainland Avebury ley web. In Godshill village, the old church stands on top of a hill. The original plan was to erect the church in the south-west of the village: the site was prepared, the stones piled up and the markers set out. But during the night all the pegs and markers were moved and arranged on top of the hill. The local bishop ordered the stones to be restored to the original site, but at midnight they were seen rolling of their own volition to the top of the hill, where the church was eventually built. It was believed that the fairies had moved them because the original site was on their path or meeting place. Painted on the wall of the church is a unique fifteenth-century representation of Christ crucified on a living tree, perhaps a relic of former tree worship.

FAIRIES AND EARTH LIGHTS

Earth lights are glowing, changing circles that either hover or whirl through the skies. They may measure only a few centimetres across, but the largest reported ones are several metres in diameter. In the daytime they are perceived as metallic or black circles. Some UFO sightings may in fact be large earth lights.

Earth lights are an ancient phenomenon and are accepted as quite normal by indigenous people such as the Native North Americans, who interpret them as manifestations of the Earth Mother. They have frequently been associated with fairy folk, as in the modern Druidic experience from Ireland mentioned in Chapter 3. Theosophists have described fairy beings as essentially glowing balls with a pinpoint of light at the centre, and earth lights and fairy sightings go hand in hand. This description is remarkably similar to the way young Andrew saw his fairies (in Chapter 3). In the Peak District in Derbyshire, England, earth lights have been seen for centuries. They are called the Longdendale Lights, after the name of the valley, but are more popularly known as the Devil's Bonfires. Some say they are the torches of Roman legions whose spirits cross the moor on the night of the first full moon in spring, but others regard them as the lights of fairy folk. Both theories are quite compatible in view of the belief that the Celtic Underworld sheltered both those who had died and those who had never possessed mortal bodies.

A hill called Lantern Pike, 10 miles (16 kilometres) to the south-west, is the home of an archetypal hag, Peggy wi' th' Lantern. According to folklore she swings her lamp on the hilltop, causing a phenomenon that has been witnessed by local residents for hundreds of years.

WILL O' THE WISPS

In northern European folklore, earth lights are also referred to as will o' the wisps. In Sweden they are known as *lykt-gubbe*, which means 'the old man with the lamp'. These flickering lights are usually seen in groups and float just above the ground. One explanation is that they are malevo-lent fairies who guard lost treasure and lead travellers astray across marshland and lonely moorlands. Others say the lumi-nous creatures actually help lost travellers, and for this reason in some regions they are called Jack o' Lanterns, giving their name to the turnip carved in the shape of a face that is placed in windows on Halloween to protect the household from harm. Yet other authorities identify the lights as those of fairy revels.

According to scientists from Isaac Newton onwards, the flame-like phosphorescence floating over marshy ground is due to the spontaneous combustion of decaying vegetable matter. But research undertaken in 1980 by Dr Alan Mills of Leicester University's Department of Geology was unable to reproduce under laboratory conditions a will o' the wisp-type flame by the spontaneous combustion of methane, phosphene and other hypothesised marshland gases. Nor could the researcher discover any natural source of ignition. Moreover, the lights are most frequently reported over mountain tops and on moorlands, rather than on marshes.

Recent projected links between earth lights and geological faults, like the spontaneous combustion theory, fail to explain the interaction between the earth lights and their perceivers. Folk tales recount how the lights beckon travellers and continue to change direction, pausing if the person following them stops. The interactive nature of earth lights was confirmed by a study carried out in 1994 in the Hessdalen valley, 70 miles (110 kilometres) south-east of Trondheim in Norway. Here, the lights actually seemed to read the thoughts of the investigators and responded to them.

Earth lights also hover over ancient stones, especially on the old festivals. At Avebury Ring, they have been perceived in accounts spanning centuries as small, luminous figures dancing around the stones just above the ground. What is fascinating is that earth lights do often appear near places where UFO sightings have been reported, especially where these are close to sacred sites, most notably in Wiltshire in England.

ARCHETYPAL EARTH SPIRITS

The Green Man/Jack i' the Green

The Green Man, known also as the Hidden One and the Wild Herdsman, is the archetypal spirit of plants, trees and vegetables, fruit and greenery. He predates formal religion and even perhaps the Horned God, consort of the Mother Goddess, with whom he has close associations.

First depicted in his present form in the Classical world, the Green Man is credited with rain-making powers and has survived in folk song, celebrations such as May Day, and in Romany lore. His image appears carved or sculpted in many churches and cathedrals, usually positioned on a ley line close to one of the Christianised goddess wells. For example, the Green Man in Minster Abbey in Kent is on a path directly between two of the three goddess wells excavated in the area by the archaeologist Brian Slade. The fearsome face of the Green Man is sometimes, especially in folk dances, covered entirely with leaves, traditionally those of the oak. Many of the Green Man stone or wood carvings in religious buildings are from the medieval period when ancient pagan symbols were regarded as protective against evil, as are his images on

numerous stained glass windows and illuminated manu-
scripts.

In spite of attempts to suppress the image at the time of
the Reformation, the Green Man survived as a folk motif. At
Maytime, especially in eastern Europe, a man dressed from
head to foot in greenery may lead the relics of ancient fertility rites. In both southern and eastern Europe, the Romany
spring festival centred around the Green Man or Green
George. A gypsy clad in greenery would play Green George
and represent the rebirth of spring after the death of winter.

In some gypsy communities on St George's Day, 23 April,
or sometimes Easter Monday, a young willow or birch tree
was cut down and dressed with flowers and ribbons.
Accompanied by Green George, it was taken to a river and
thrown in as a substitute for Green George, to appease the
water spirits and ensure there would be enough rain to bring
a good harvest.

In a similar but female-focused ritual, at Whitsun in
Russia and other Slavic lands a birch tree is dressed in
women's clothing to welcome the coming of summer.

The origins of this archetypal male Earth Force are uncertain. He is akin to the ancient Horned God, the son/consort
of the Mother Goddess and Lord of the Hunt. The Celts had
the horned Cerunnos as their earth deity. Among the Saxons
he was Herne the Hunter, the antlered God of the Forest. In
the very ancient myths, the old god as King Stag was
defeated by the new young king each year. This is the origin
of the sacrifice ritual that is central to most religions, particularly those involving the Corn Gods.

In Classical times Pan, the wild fairy/deity of the groves

of Arcadia, was the herdsman's god and was seen as half goat. From his father Hermes, the Greek messenger god, Pan inherited his gift for music, and he created the pan pipes that are now enjoying a revival. Yet he was not an immortal and was not allowed on Mount Olympus. He was too untamed and untameable even for the liberal Greek pantheon. In the secret magical traditions of the early twentieth-century esoteric societies, the invocation of Pan summoned his wildness back into a world grown stagnant and over-sophisticated.

Robin Hood of the greenwood was also regarded as an archetypal being, clad in the green of the fairy people and totally unrelated to the outlaw tales. Little John was Janus, the two-headed god, and Maid Marian the maiden goddess. The Pied Piper of Hamelin, immortalised in Robert Browning's poem, was another form of the archetypal Earth Spirit, a Pan figure who led the children of the town into a green hill that closed behind them.

In *Faery Wicca* Star Hawk, author of *The Spiral Dance* and many other books, healer, eco-warrior and white witch who has done much to open up the field of magic to lay people, described the three gods of Faery Wicca. All related to aspects of the self and born of the Virgin Goddess, they are the Blue God of gentleness and love, the Green God of the plant world, and the White-Horned God of the animals, the wild hunter.

SPRING-HEELED JACK, A MODERN ARCHETYPE OF EARTH ENERGIES

The modern Green Man is the terrifying figure known as Spring-heeled Jack. He is described as a spectre who leaps upon his unsuspecting victims before bounding away with huge leaps. According to witnesses, he is dressed in a skin-tight suit, has protruding eyes and is able to jump up to 30 feet (10 metres) in height in a single bound. Jack's appearances have spanned nearly two centuries, beginning in 1817, and descriptions have ranged from a monster with wings and horns to a powerfully built demonic man with a helmet and cloak, spitting fire.

I use the present tense when describing Spring-heeled Jack because his last appearance was only a few years ago. Mark Fraser, Editor of *Haunted Scotland* and a paranormal investigator, collected an account from George, an ex-army officer who now works as a salesman and who encountered Spring-heeled Jack in the summer of 1986. George was in south Herefordshire, riding along a quiet country road not far from the Welsh border. A movement in the field to his left caught his eye and he was astounded to see a strange figure of a man physically leaping high hedgerows in great bounds, as though he was gliding above the ground and defying the laws of gravity.

Suddenly the man leaped on to the road and, as he glided

past George, slapped him so hard across the face that George fell to the ground and was left with the red imprint on his cheek for several hours. Spring-heeled Jack gave out an almighty cackle of a laugh and carried on with his journey across the fields. It all happened so fast that George was dumbstruck. He later described Jack as wearing a black all-in-one suit and having an elongated chin.

The report bears a remarkable similarity to earlier reports of Jack, a character who travelled far and wide. Sightings were especially numerous in the Midlands, the Home Counties and as far north as Cheshire and Lancashire.

Barnes Common in London was a favourite haunt, and in Victorian times when he was first sighted there it was still deep in the countryside. In September 1837, a businessman crossed the common late at night on his way home. Suddenly a figure with pointed ears, glowing eyes and a long nose vaulted over the high railings of a cemetery and landed in front of him. The businessman fled, but the same night a butcher was found murdered on Barnes Common and it was said that for years afterwards no grass would grow on the spot where the body had been found.

According to a Hampshire witness on another occasion, Jack possessed huge ears and a tail, so it might be that he was able to shape-shift. In February 1838, Lucy Scales and her sister Margaret were walking home through Limehouse in the East End of London when at the entrance to the aptly named Green Dragon Alley Jack, wearing a cloak, leaped out of the darkness, breathing a jet of blue flames from his mouth that temporarily blinded Lucy. Significantly she was not burned – a tribute to Jack's power of illusion. Margaret watched Jack escape by leaping on to the roof of a house.

Clearly the timescale, the amazing gymnastic feats and the many different descriptions suggest that Jack was not mortal. My own belief is that he was some kind of personification of earth energies, perhaps fuelled by a form of earth power. It could be that all his appearances were on or close to old leys that still run beneath towns as well as through the country-side. Did he draw power from his victims like a psychic vampire? Certainly his appearances would suggest that there are creatures linked to the Earth who, like the Green Man, defy categorisation. Jack, the latter-day Green Man, is one of the most fascinating and thought-provoking forms of the mystery.

EXERCISE: FINDING YOUR FAIRY LEY LEGENDS

You may decide to spend a few days in a magical area of known ley energies, for example Glastonbury, that still retains its magic in spite of commercialisation. Or you could explore your own locality, since ley lines criss-cross every area.

- Begin by purchasing a book of local legends or visiting a local library and noting down any that relate to fairies, giants or other magical beings.

- Use an Ordnance Survey Landranger series map, scale 1:50 000, for the UK, or one of a similar scale in your own country, and a metre stick to provide a straight edge.

- Begin by looking on the map for any names with obvious fairy connections, such as Puckpool, Fairy Hill or The Devil's Cauldron, and then examine the map for fairy forts which will be marked as tumuli. Look too for churches because they were often built on the sites of ancient temples, any wells or well name places such as Brideswell, standing stones, long barrows, stone circles and sacred sites. These all acted as markers on leys. (When you are walking the leys, you may add rocky outcrops and clumps of hawthorns, until recently tended by an earthly guardian, and large pools.)

- See if you can draw a straight line through at least five such landmarks, and if so you can be fairly sure you have hit a ley. There are books about ley lines in many local regions, but it is always fun to find your own.

- Now see where your legends fit, and you will probably discover that many are close to the projected ley. Sometimes you will get a fearsome giant story where two leys cross.

- Next walk part of your ley. This is the only way to experience, for example, standing on a fairy fort, and seeing how the leys radiate over the land. You may even see lines of sparkling sunlight. Let your feet guide you and ignore logic, for today for you are using quite a different part of your mind.

- Visit the spots mentioned in the old stories and try to find the place where the fairies held their revels. Track down the fountain of youth, the magical well in the forest or the circle of Druidesses who were turned to stone by an early saint for dancing on the Sabbath. The best way to experience the power is to feel it beneath your feet.

- Reread the stories at the elfin glade or witch tree. Children love such outings more than the most expensive artificial magical kingdom.

- Walk the sacred glades, dance the circles, hear the old voices carried on the wind and experience real magic.

- When you get home, plot your leys and mark in the legends you relived.

- Wherever you go on holiday, you can begin at a sacred site and explore the true America, Spain or Turkey. You may discover, as I did, that the ley you are treading extends hundreds if not thousands of miles. The ley line I found at Mont St Michel on the borders of Normandy and Brittany in France begins at Mount Carmel in Israel and runs through Avebury right to the east coast of England; along it ranged tales of dragons, fairies, pixies, black elemental dogs, well maidens, enchanted islands, avenging angels, sun deities and subterranean entrances into the Otherworld.

CHAPTER EIGHT
The Darker Side of Fairies

Up the airy mountain,
Down the rushy glen,
We daren't go a-hunting
For fear of little men;

'The Fairies', WILLIAM ALLINGHAM (1824–1889)

Mortals sometimes project what they fear most on to creatures of the night or hideous monsters. Therefore the fairy kingdom has more than its share of ugly trolls, giants and hags. The hags are discussed in Chapter 9, on powerful fairies, since they are sources of great power which can transform the old into the new, the stagnant into the innovative. Of course, it can be terrifying for gallant knights when the lovely fairy they think they are seducing reveals her bad hair day hag form at the crucial point of passion or, as with Perrault's Sleeping Beauty's mother-in-law, turns out to be an ogress, intent on devouring the fair somnambulist.

However, though there are inevitably some thoroughly nasty specimens in the fairy kingdom just as there are in the human world, it is often the size or ugliness that defines the villains in the cosmic story.

FAIRIES AND THE WORLD OF GHOSTS

The hardest concept to reconcile to the conventional fairy world is the repeated references in folklore of Fairyland being a place where ghosts reside, as discussed in Chapter 1. For some, the Celtic Otherworld concept sits uneasily with the more conventional religious view of the virtuous up in Heaven and the damned below in Hell or Hades.

In some cultures the ancestors may reside on top of a high mountain or in a forest; in some African nations the ancestors continue life in villages under the ground, connected to this world by holes allowing visits by the living. Wealthy Ancient Egyptians were buried with servants or statues of them so that they might continue to till the land and care for the deceased in the next world. It is only in sky god religions that Heaven becomes associated with bliss and the underworld is a dark, sad region occupied by shades. Though I have studied and written about the Celtic Land of Youth, where dead and living mingle, on a personal level I have found it a hard concept to reconcile with my early upbringing as a

High Anglican. Yet if it is our spirit or etheric bodies that survive death and are the part that travels to Fairyland during a person's lifetime, and fairies are composed of similar etheric material, then it should perhaps not be surprising that the two mingle.

Fairy Dogs

The wildest of the creatures belonging to the fairies, fairy dogs have become the focus of legends as their innate untamability became translated into demonic qualities.

Black Shuck is the most dramatic of the huge black fairy dogs that have, according to local folk lore, roamed the countryside of East Anglia, Scotland, the North of England and the Isle of Man throughout history. Like other fairy dogs, for example Black Angus in Scotland, Shuck is said to herald death within the year to anyone he encounters. He has been described as being as 'big as a calf with saucer sized eyes that glow yellow or red'. The phenomenon of howling devil dogs has inspired many books, films and plays, including Conan Doyle's *Hound of the Baskervilles*.

The Shuck stories probably derive from Viking invaders who brought legends of Odin's black hounds and Thor's dog, Shukr.

THE WILD HUNT

One of the most fascinating concepts is that of the Wild Hunt – at certain times of the year the spirits ride through the air with ghosts, fairies and witches. The Wild Hunt led by

Gwynn ap Nudd, the White One, the fairy king who guarded the portal on Glastonbury Tor, was mentioned earlier.

Original reports of the Wild Hunt tell of sky or woodland hunts led by a pagan deity, but the demonic aspect of ghostly riders seeking the souls of the living was emphasised by the monks who recorded the old legends. This slant not only fuelled fear of the old gods but served as an explanation for the disappearance without trace of people in wild country places. It is not so many hundreds of years since wild animals roamed freely in Europe, Scandinavia and North America. Even in the nineteenth century, bands of brigands who preyed on travellers, as well as vampires and werewolves, were still accepted as reality.

The Viking Odin (Woden in the Anglo-Saxon tradition) was regarded as one of the original leaders of the Wild Hunt in Scandinavia, Germany and the north and east of England. Originally, however, Odin chased wood elves, sometimes beautiful maidens, or in England a white stag. At the Midwinter Solstice he dropped gifts at the foot of his sacred pine for the faithful – one of the origins of Christmas presents. Odin's eight-legged horse Sleipnir was the source of the legend of the eight reindeer of Santa Claus. Santa himself was the old Holly King/Odin and St Nicholas rolled into one. When Odin was demonised (he can still be seen in his devilish persona as Black Peter or Black Rupert in St Nicholas Day processions in Europe) his huntsmen and women became the ungodly dead. Unable to gain admission to heaven, they were released from Hell to hunt for – what else but souls?

In Scotland, the Slaugh who were in the original folklore part of the Seelie Court became the Wild Hunt of sinners who flew through the skies at midnight, kidnapping unsuspecting travellers out late at night whose only chance of escape was to cling to the trees and bushes as the whirlwind passed overhead. They were also said to fly in from the west to capture a dying soul before it was shriven. For this reason, as late as the early twentieth century in Scotland doors and windows on the west side of the house were kept closed to keep the huntsmen away (see also Chapter 2).

A Saxon version of the Wild Hunt mythology in England identifies the leader as Herne the Hunter, a form of the ancient Horned God (see Chapter 7) whose hunt takes place in the wild woods. The Christianised twelfth-century *Anglo-Saxon Chronicles* describe the black hunters and hounds, the hunters mounted on black horses and goats, blowing their horns of doom.

In northern Italy the shamanic Benandanti, meaning 'good walkers' or 'good-doers', followers of Diana and members of a fertility cult, traditionally left their bodies on the four Ember days. These were religious days at the beginning of each of the four seasons, associated with prayer and fasting but originally pagan celebrations of nature. In their astral forms the Benandanti fought sky battles against the Malandanti – evil witches, demons and spirits – to ensure the safety of the harvest and their villages. They rode, armed with fennel stalks, sometimes in the form of animals themselves, on cats, goats and horses to ensure the safety of the crops. During the Wild Hunt, the Benandanti also kept the paths of the dead from this world to the next secure. Although they fought on the side of the angels, the Benandanti were regarded by the sixteenth-century Inquisition as evil. However, in spite of persecution the tradition continued, and may still do so in secret.

FAIRIES AND WITCHES

During the witchcraft trials that reached their height in Europe between the fifteenth and seventeenth centuries, witches sometimes confessed under torture to have consorted with fairies who became associated with the Devil. The simple explanation may be that ordinary people – midwives, herbalists and those against whom neighbours bore grudges – who knew nothing of witchcraft and were falsely accused were well versed in fairy lore, and so might include details of fairy/demonic visitations in order to satisfy the Inquisitors.

But even those who did belong to a coven of nature worshippers, who were often initiated by a grey or dark man, probably a coven master rather than an otherworldly demon, would associate magic with fairies. Though they were consorting with the fairies, who in the Inquisitors' minds were demonic, true Devil worshippers were usually either master magicians or dispossessed clergy and had no time for the fairy folk.

The most famous witchcraft trial to which fairies were central was that of Isobel Gowdie and Janet Breadheid from Nairn in Scotland in 1662. Most unusually, Isobel made her confessions entirely voluntarily – it has been suggested that she was a bored wife who craved excitement and notoriety.

Both women were initiated by a grey man dressed in black, a fairy devil described by Isobel as 'meikle, roch. Blak man, cloven footed'. She spoke of the fairy devils who led other local covens, but they were dressed in yellow and green, the fey colours. Isobel told how she rode to the coven on a little magic horse or flew, like the other witches, on fairy beanstalks.

She claimed she had the power to shape-shift into a hare, a crow and a cat. Isobel knew a great deal about witchcraft, but also described fairy involvement in great detail. She recounted meeting the Queen of the Fairies and visiting Fairyland, describing how 'the hills opened and we came to a large and braw room – and there I got meat from the Queen of the Faerie, more than I could eat. The Queen of the Faerie is brawly clothed in white linens – and the King of the Faerie is a braw man, well-favoured and broad-faced.'

Isobel alleged that she had witnessed the Devil himself in Fairyland making elf bolts, the legendary flint arrows that were shot without bows, and claimed to have killed a woman using one. She also said she had seen fearsome fairy bulls. Like the majority of those who confessed to witchcraft both Isobel and Janet were convicted and executed.

Another witch, Bessie Dunlop, who was condemned in 1576, told of a fairy friend, Thom Reid, another grey man. She claimed she had been visited in childbirth by the Queen of Elfhame, who had told her that her child would die but that her sick husband would live. Both events came true.

CHANGELINGS

One of the most serious accusations made against fairies, and a source of countless legends, is the changeling phenomenon whereby fairies and elves stole babies and substituted one of their own in the cradle. (Of course, as devil's advocate one might argue that humans quite commonly stole sealskins or swan cloaks to capture fairies and compel them to become mortal brides, and that a number of the young people supposedly restored from Fairyland to their former homes were not at all happy to return to a life of deprivation and hard toil after feasting and luxury.)

In *A Midsummer Night's Dream* Puck described one such abduction. He says:

> *The King doth keep his revels here tonight,*
> *Take heed the Queen come not within his sight,*
> *For Oberon is passing fell and wrath,*
> *Because she as her attendant hath*
> *A lovely boy, stol'n from an Indian King,*
> *She never had so sweet a changeling,*
> *And jealous Oberon would have the child,*
> *Knight of his train to trace the forests wild:*
> *But she perforce withholds the loved boy,*
> *Crowns him with flowers and makes him all her joy.*

It was said that fairies might cast glamour over the changeling to make it appear identical to the missing baby. If it was a fairy child the infant might be unduly precocious, and, when apparently unobserved, climb out of its cradle and walk or talk while still very young. Physically and intellectually advanced mortal children were therefore regarded with suspicion, especially in a small community where the parents were servants or farm workers.

In other cases, the fairies might cast enchantment over a block of wood to make it seem like the child they had snatched. In such cases, a previously healthy young child might overnight become sickly and weak, or die without warning. This was, as suggested earlier, a way for parents to deal with their grief when, as happened so often, a child died of natural causes. They would console themselves that their true child was in Fairyland.

However, the majority of accounts describe the changeling as a wizened, misshapen baby, hairy and with a monstrous head. It was said to eat ravenously but never grow (or, if it grew, to be horribly deformed) and to cry continually.

Folklore offers various remedies to make the ever-crying changeling laugh or to trick it into revealing its true age and identity. The story of the soldier and the egg exists in various versions in many parts of Europe. A soldier returns home from the wars to find his younger brother still in the cradle after some twenty years. The soldier empties an eggshell, fills it with water and begins heating it over a fire. The changeling asks what is happening and the soldier replies that he is brewing beer. This amuses the changeling enough for it to laugh out loud and say: 'Old, old I am, but in all my years I have never seen a soldier brewing beer in an eggshell.' The deception now revealed, the soldier attacks the changeling with a whip and it vanishes. The long-lost brother, now a grown man, is restored to the family. Other versions of the tale neglect the egg brewing and go straight into the whipping option, at which point the fairy or elf who carried out the substitution appears, crying: 'Do not attack my child for I never did yours any harm.' She then returns the missing baby.

As the concept of the changeling is so widespread in folklore, it is interesting to speculate on what basis there could be for it in reality. I asked Dr Clarke, a GP from Essex, with an interest in paranormal experiences, about the medical aspects. 'The description of a changeling is not identifiable as a particular syndrome,' he said, 'rather a series of disabilities that separately or together would mark a child as different. When parents had a child that looked unusual, one acceptable hypothesis in times past was that the Devil had got into the child somehow. Dietary shortages in times past could explain much of the lack of growth and normal development, especially in poor families. In earlier days, a high proportion of children failed to thrive and infant mortality was as high as 50–60 per cent. The changeling theory was a convenient explanation for unfortunate parents who produced a socially unacceptable child.'

For the child regarded as a changeling, life could be hard, especially if the parents decided to use the whipping method of unmasking him. In 1843 the *West Briton* newspaper reported the case of a J. Trevelyan of Penzance who was charged with ill-treating one of his children. The child was said to have been regularly beaten by his parents and their servants, and from the age of fifteen months had been left to live outside. The parents' defence was that he was not their child but a changeling, and the case against them was dismissed.

'A century and a half ago,' Dr Clarke commented, 'the railway had only just broken through to Cornwall and until then it had been virtually cut off. When Wesley [the founder of Methodism] went there in the 1780s he found a land rife with paganism and folklore. Cornwall at that time was appealingly backward, with gross poverty, great ignorance and conditions that horrified Wesley.'

Women too were abducted and taken to Fairyland, either to act as midwives to fairy women if they were old and wise, or in the case of young mothers to feed the infant fairies on the much desired human milk. Young brides were kidnapped to be impregnated and to bear fairy children. The children were either raised as mortals and possessed powerful clairvoyant powers, or would be exchanged after birth for a piece of enchanted wood.

MALEVOLENT FAIRIES

Some fairies, however, are regarded as wholly malevolent. Usually these are small, dark creatures who live underground or in wooded or lonely places, or are fiends of the night. The gremlin is found in Germany and Britain and has given his name to things that go unexpectedly wrong, especially with machinery (not to mention a series of popular films). Varying in size from human to quite tiny, gremlins are hairy and brown with malevolent smiles and come out mostly at night.

Once able to fly but now living on mountain tops, gremlins gave rise to stories during World War II that they had been seen on the wings of both German and British fighter planes, and in some cases had caused damage or terrified pilots by appearing in front of the windshield when the plane was high in the sky. In times of war and crisis, as everyday preoccupations recede, glimpses of other dimensions do become more prevalent, even among the most logical and hard-headed people.

Another fairy foe that is as inimical to other fairies as to humans is the goblin or orc of Germanic and Scandinavian origin. Goblins are small, strong, black and ugly, with eyes like glowing coals. These spiteful creatures of the night shun daylight, roam in bands, live in dark, underground places or deep forests and are often regarded as the antithesis of the elves. In Tolkien's *The Hobbit* the Goblin King captured and enslaved the dwarves and Bilbo for a time in the mines of the Misty Mountains. Goblins are notorious in folklore for capturing other fairy people and forcing them to work as slaves in their mines.

Goblins are great shape-shifters but, true to kind, turn into wild animals, bats or owls. They terrify and harass travellers and children (see the case study of Ivy in Chapter 3). Goblins are also associated with the darker side of

Halloween, their special festival when they roam unchecked over the Earth.

Their dark image has rubbed off on to their harmless kin, the hobgoblin, a domestic spirit first referred to as demonic in John Bunyan's hymn 'To Be a Pilgrim': 'Hobgoblin nor foul fiend shall daunt thy spirit.' The hob or hearth goblin was more akin to a brownie, though uglier and without fingers or toes. It was the more negative image of the hobgoblin that travelled to America with the Pilgrim Fathers and, over the years, the hobgoblin has lived up to his bad image.

However, some apparently malevolent creatures are in fact protective of a particular species or place, and will only do harm when humans pose a threat. For example, the Cururipur, a South American spirit and lord of the jungle, protects tortoises as his special creatures, attacking all who would do them harm.

THE POWER OF NATURE – THE BIG BEINGS

Most of the bad guys of the magical kingdoms are regarded as threatening because of their sheer size, which obviously makes for a fair amount of destruction even on a gentle walk-about. Just as small races of people became associated with fairies, so did tall races become known as giants. Originally, when people lived in caves, huts or open spaces, these giant beings were regarded as Creator Spirits, who came from the skies and their presence was considered a blessing, but once houses and towns hampered the giants' free access over the terrain they became enemies of mankind. Especially so was the ogre, an ugly, slightly smaller, cannibalistic cousin of the gentle giant, with an unfortunate habit of tearing up trees and hurling rocks if annoyed. One of the few positive giant stories is Oscar Wilde's *The Selfish Giant*, the tale of a creature who tore down the walls of his garden to admit a poor ragged child to enter and so restored spring to it.

Celtic giants

The Formorians, the giants said to have oppressed the people of Ireland, were defeated by the Tuatha de Danaan, and so, like all defeated peoples, were recorded for posterity in a wholly negative way. In the mythological cycles written by the early monastic scribes the main tale is of the Battle of Moytura (Cath Maig Tuired), the final conflict between the Tuatha de Danaan, the People of the goddess Dana, and the Formorians.

There are various interpretations of this decisive battle in which all the Irish deities took part. The conventional one depicts it as a straightforward struggle of good against evil. And so, since the Tuatha de Danaan were very beautiful, the bad guys were inevitably portrayed as half-monsters, hideous and misshapen, with a single hand, foot and eye. However, matters may have been less clear-cut and the Battle of Moytura a struggle between the old order of gods and the new, between Blar or Balor, the old God of Light, and a new solar god, Lug Samildanach. A third view sees it as a battle between the priest and warrior classes, the Tuatha de Danaan, and the farmers, the providers.

Viking giants

In Viking mythology, giants were also the enemies of the gods. However, because of their vital role in the creation myths their realm, Jotunheim, was on the uppermost level of Yggdrassil, the World Tree, parallel with Asgard, home of the gods.

In Norse mythology, ice from Niflheim in the north and fire from Muspellheim in the south fused in the vast chasm of Ginnungagap, bringing forth life. The first two beings were Ymir the frost giant and Audumla, the primal cow/mother. Audumla licked a pillar of salt ice and brought forth Buri, the first of the gods, who married the giantess Bestia. She gave birth to three sons who became the gods of the Aesir, Odin (spirit), Vili (will) and Ve (holiness), or according to some versions Odin, Hoenir (the Shining One) and Loki, the Trickster, God of Fire. The gods fought with the frost giants and eventually killed Ymir.

From Ymir's body the gods created the nine worlds that were supported by the World Tree, a gigantic ash. From his hair the woods were formed and from his blood the waters of the Earth. Unfortunately, as with the Formorians, the Norse giants' overthrow by the gods of the Aesir resulted in their being cast into the villains' role.

Another creator tale is of the giant who took up a handful of soil, so creating Lake Vaner, the largest lake in Europe. Where he threw down the soil in the Baltic Sea Gotland was formed, a region that still possesses a rich folk tradition.

The builder giants

There are various Scandinavian legends that tell of giants who have assisted with the building of great cathedrals and churches. Perhaps the most famous story is of the giant Finn who built the cathedral at Lund in the southern Swedish province of Skane. In May 2000, I visited this magnificent building which has successfully reconciled the new religion with the old ways. On an astrological clock within the cathedral Saturn and the Three Wise men co-exist quite happily.

The legend, told from the Christian point of view, was that a family of giants lived in Helgonabacken, the hills of Helgona, and were very upset that the holy man Laurentius had arrived in the area and intended to erect a cathedral. However, a local giant offered to do the building and asked in return that the saint should guess his name. This was a common demand, for such names were carefully guarded since to know the name of a magical being was to gain power over it. If he could not guess the name, the giant said, Laurentius must give him the sun and moon.

Laurentius offered instead his eyes if he could not guess the name – perhaps an unwise bargain for free labour. Before long the giant had completed the entire church except for the final stone on the tower. The previous day Laurentius, after various unsuccessful guesses at the giant's name, went walking on Helgonabacken, realising that the giant would soon ask for his eyes. Suddenly he heard a child crying from inside the hill and the child's mother soothing it, saying, 'Hush, little one, for tomorrow your father Finn will return either with the sun and moon or the holy man's eyes.'

Laurentius hurried back to the church and called, 'Finn,

for Finn you are, though of no name in the eyes of the Lord, unblest as you are except by your heathen gods.'

Finn was so angry that he seized one of the pillars and shook it in an attempt to make the church collapse. Hearing the shouting, Finn's wife rushed to the church and began to help her husband. However, both giants and the child were turned to stone, it is said by the angels. The figures can be seen in the crypt clinging to pillars, the wife still holding her baby.

Such legends are relatively common in Scandinavia. For example, a troll was said to have assisted St Olaf with the building of the church in Norrland in Sweden. They are strange tales, saying more perhaps about the establishment of a new religion and the destruction of the old. When I saw the pillars in Lund, I felt a stirring of pity for Finn's innocent baby who was also turned to stone, cradled so lovingly by his mother.

FIERCE CREATURES

Trolls

Belief in the existence of trolls is perhaps higher than for many fairy beings. In modern times they are, however, rarely seen, except in deep forests or mountainous regions by local people, to whom they are like any other rare forest creature and definitely off limits. Scandinavian and German folklore is full of tales of wicked trolls, although they have become more human-friendly in recent years in the form of a very popular toy, dressed for any role from a US marine to a Bride.

Though trolls come in different sizes, many are large. All are characterised by grotesque, fleshy faces and hairy, stocky bodies, huge hands, feet, noses and ears and bushy tails, with a reputation for ill temper and fierceness. It is said that fierce giants called Jotuns (or *jætter* in Danish) were the ancestors of Scandinavian trolls. According to legend, these giant trolls settled in the far north after the final Ice Age, but became extinct as people moved to remoter parts.

Norwegian trolls now live in caves in mountains along the fjords. These trolls were immortalised in Henrik Ibsen's play *Peer Gynt*, published in 1867, and especially in the music of Edvard Grieg with such evocative pieces as 'In the Hall of the Mountain King' (written as incidental music for Ibsen's play) that captured the magnificence of the trolls' underground world.

The Gotland *trull* resides in ancient burial mounds or stone cairns and frequently moves house. The smaller Scandinavian forest troll, Skovtrold or Skogstroll, who is closer to a dwarf or gnome in size, occupies remoter Swedish and Finnish forests and feeds mainly on mushrooms and toadstools. Trolls also appear in northern Scotland, especially in the Shetlands where they are known as trows or hill trows, and in northern Italy.

It is believed that, like dwarves and gnomes, many trolls cannot stand strong sunshine. However, their underground dwellings may have more to do with earlier persecutions by humans, and some trolls seem actively to seek winter sunlight. At the Autumn Equinox trolls of all kinds congregate at ancient sites such as dolmens. It has been said that the trolls represented an amoral, self-centred world, although Peer Gynt was happy enough to go along with his marriage to a troll bride and live in the underground caverns until he realised that the troll princess in her true form was unlikely to win any beauty contests.

Why are trolls reviled? Primarily because of their ugliness, for stories do filter through of trolls helping animals and travellers and being wise in herb lore. Generally hostile to humans, perhaps because their ancestors were driven out by settlers, trolls are natural guardians of bridges and highways and as such are very territorial.

A strange story that reveals a vulnerability in trolls comes from Gotland. It concerns the Torespieskot, a troll-like creature who may take the form of an old woman, a magpie or a sheep. According to local tradition, the Torespieskot is afraid of thunder because she lives in terror of the ancient god Thor and his thunderbolts. Therefore she would knock on doors seeking shelter during a storm.

For this reason people in Gotland would place crosses at their windows and scissors at their door to repel the troll. One story tells of a farmer's wife who sat sewing at her open door when it began to thunder. An old woman came, begging for shelter, but when she saw the scissors and needles asked the farmer's wife to take them away. Recognising a Torespieskot, the farmer's wife told the troll to shelter in a nearby oak tree, a naturally protective tree against storms. However, lightning struck the tree and the troll was destroyed.

EXERCISE: REDUCING THE POWER OF THE GIANT

Giants hold great power both psychologically and psychically, but this may be locked up in a form that evokes fear of
being overwhelmed and crushed. If, however, the power can
be transformed into positive energy and released slowly, the
giant can be a welcome source of power to any person's life.

- First create your giant or gigantic troll. If you are expert at
  computing you can use a Paint or Draw program to create
  your giant on screen.

- If not, draw or paint one on paper. In either case endow the
  giant or troll with all the characteristics you fear/dislike in
  yourself or in those around you or in people from the past
  whose influence still worries you. For example, if a former
  partner/parent unfairly accused you of extravagance or was
  excessively mean, you might weight the giant's neck down
  with gold rings or fill his hands with money bags from which
  coins were spilling. If you really hate your appearance/have
  been told by a super-critical friend or spiteful ex-lover you
  were ugly/fat, give your giant a huge nose, flapping ears and
  perhaps an exaggerated stomach, so he/she really has taken
  on all the imagined ugliness that has wounded your self-
  esteem. If you are repressing anger, he can breathe fire or
  have a mighty sword. You may find that your giant bears a
  resemblance to an autocratic boss or overbearing relation.

- Write words or phrases across the giant if you wish, maybe
  undeserved criticism or scorn that years later still hurt – it is

your personal giant and can be as idiosyncratic as you wish. Make the symbols as outrageous as you like.

- Now begin either to delete or to block out with dark colour parts of your giant, beginning with those that trouble you most. For each segment removed, write on a separate screen/paper a strength that is the antidote of a particular negativity – for instance, for 'meanness' write in gigantic letters 'generosity' or 'giver of abundance'.

- When you have finished you should have a satisfyingly empty screen or sheet of paper and a whole series of power words. Keep your list and add to it regularly. If your self-esteem feels low at a future time, create another giant and recycle positive energies into your world.

CHAPTER NINE

The Powerful Fairies

In the morning of life came the good fairy with her
basket and said:
'Here are gifts. Take one, leave the others.
And be wary, choose wisely; oh, choose wisely!
for only one of them is valuable.'
The gifts were five: Fame, Love, Riches,
Pleasure, Death.

The Five Boons of Life, MARK TWAIN (1835–1910)

Many of the fairy kings and queens have their roots in pre-Christian religion. They represent the same attributes and strengths, albeit diluted, as the original deity forms. In Fairyland, they may be rulers of the fairy nobility or separate but powerful entities who appear to mortals at times such as death or birth when the dimensions move closer.

THE FATES

The Goddesses of Fate, usually three sisters who are weavers or spinners of the web of destiny, are central to many mythologies. Always above and beyond the power of even the Sky Fathers and the parameters of accepted time, they represent unanswerable questions that lie at the heart of spirituality. They may be found throughout fairy mythology as the Fairy Godmother/wicked fairy, especially at a birth when they endow the hero or heroine with a blueprint of his or her future destiny.

In the Fairy Godmother/wise woman role they intervene on the hero/heroine's behalf in times of crisis. But for every Fairy Godmother who gives the ragged Cinderella the impetus to challenge the status quo there is a wicked witch. In Shakespeare's *Macbeth* it is three wicked witches, who point out to the hero possibilities of attaining his heart's desire through his own wicked deeds and the option of blaming it all on fate.

First Witch: All hail, Macbeth! hail to thee, thane of Glamis!
Second Witch: All hail, Macbeth! hail to thee, thane of Cawdor!
Third Witch: All hail, Macbeth, that shalt be king hereafter!

THE VIKING CONCEPT OF FATE

The Norns are three sisters, none other than Macbeth's Weird or *Wyrd* Sisters who wove the web both of the world and of the fate of individual beings, mortal and gods. They wove, not according to their own desires, but according to Orlog, the eternal law of the universe.

The Teutonic concept of destiny was a forerunner of the modern idea that each human being influences his or her fate by what he or she is, does and has been. So destiny is not fixed but constantly changing, as we take the magic key or potion or, as in Macbeth's case, the short cut to the top job.

Their almost imperceptible transition to Fairy God-mother/bad fairy can be seen clearly in a tale of how the three Fates or Norns once visited Denmark and went to the house of a nobleman whose wife had just given birth to their first child. The first Norn promised that the boy would grow to be brave and strong, and the second that he would become rich and be a great poet. But the third Norn was accidentally pushed out of the way by neighbours and angrily declared that the child would live only until the taper at the bedside was burned through.

Seeing the mother's distress, the second Norn blew out the taper and gave it to the weeping mother, saying that it should never be lit until her son wearied of life. The other predictions came true for Nornagesta, as the boy was called. After his parents' death Nornagesta kept the taper in the frame of his harp and for three hundred years fought bravely and sang great songs, never getting older. At last he went to the court of King Olaf Tryggvesson, who insisted the poet was baptised. As a sign of his new faith, Nornagesta lit the taper. When it burned through, he died.

There is a more doom-laden version from the north of Scotland in which three fairy women enter the house of a newborn child. A burning ember falls on to the hearth and burns one of the fairy women, who declares that when the coal is burned through the child will die. The good fairy part is taken by a midwife or old nurse, who extinguishes the ember, wraps it in linen and gives it to the mother, who locks it in a box. The baby girl grows up beautiful and clever, but on the eve of her wedding finds the box and, thinking it is a gift, prises it open – in some versions she finds a rusty key. Believing the coal may contain fairy gold or a precious gem, she throws it on the fire and so fulfils the prophecy. Here harsh fate and circumstance do over-ride free will – a sharp reminder that, while we can influence fate by the choices we make, as Macbeth and Cinderella did, sometimes what seems to be blind fortune or misfortune can intervene. The fey universe is no more tidy and free from contradictions than the mortal world.

THE MOERAE OR MOIRAI

This has become a generic term for Greek fairies, formerly three shadowy deities of Fate, who still maintain an interest in the lives of children and so are welcomed into homes. They are sometimes seen as three middle-aged women. In the original Clotho wove the thread of life, Lachesis measured it out and Atropos cut it off with her scissors of death. The Roman Fates were very similar. Called the Parcae, three very old women spin the fate of mortal destiny. Nona spun the thread of life, Decuma assigned it to a person and Morta cut it, ending that person's life.

THE HAGS

Closely linked with the fairies of destiny are the Crone Goddesses who appear as hags in fairy tales. In the legends of eastern Europe and Scandinavia the old hag is not a wicked witch *per se*, but retains the transformative powers of the Hag Goddesses and is a dispenser of justice. The famous iron-toothed fairy hag from the Russian tradition, Baba Yaga, lived in a hut that danced on giant chicken legs and was surrounded by a fence made of human bones (perhaps a remnant of the Death or Bone Goddess who re-formed the dead into a more perfect form. She rode through the skies in a mortar and pestle and was benevolent, although still terrifying, towards the deserving, but harsh to those who had done evil or been selfish.

In one story a young girl called Lubachka was hated by her stepmother, who, in the father's absence, sent the girl to Baba Yaga's house to ask for fire for the family hearth. Fortunately her aunt gave Lubachka magical items which allowed her to fulfil the tasks asked of her by Baba Yaga and escape, stealing the fire. In a second and probably older version, Vasalisa, protected by a talismanic magic doll her mother had given her before her death, was sent to Baba Yaga for a piece of coal to restore the fire and was rewarded for her efforts with a blazing skull. However, it also burned her wicked stepmother and step-sister to death. As in all good fairy tales, the father, who had absented himself when matters became troublesome, accepted the sudden change of domestic arrangements and was as happily cared for by his daughter as he had been by his new wife.

CELTIC HAGS – THE CAILLEACHS

These fairy hags, whose generic name, Cailleach, means the Veiled One, were once powerful goddesses. They are still expert shape-shifters who can assume the form of lovely maidens, hares, cats, stones and, like the Old Hag of

Rollright (see Chapter 5), trees.

One of the most fascinating is the Scottish Cailleac Bhuer, the Blue Hag, an old woman wearing black or dark blue rags with a crow on her left shoulder and a holly staff that can kill a mortal with a touch. She roams the Highlands by night during winter when her power is at its greatest. As the old hag of winter, at midnight on May Eve she casts her staff under a holly bush and is turned to stone until six months later, on Halloween, she rises again. Cailleac Bhuer is credited with creating the mountains by flying through the sky dropping stones, said by some folklorists to be the origin of the nursery rhyme 'There was an old woman tossed up in a basket.'

THE BANSHEES – HERALDS OF DEATH

Chapter 3 mentioned the banshees of West Virginia, who had travelled with settlers from their original homes in Ireland and Scotland. The banshees and other fairy goddesses that warn of death are part of a very old tradition, rooted in the belief that the Great Mother, sometimes in the form of the Moon Mother, absorbed the souls of the departed to await rebirth. Part of the Celtic Otherworld was the Land of Women, mentioned in Chapter 2.

The fairy washerwomen

One of the most fascinating forms of banshee are the fairy washerwomen of Brittany, *les lavandières de nuit*, who haunt the ancient wash-houses like those beneath the walls of Vannes, an ancient fortified city in southern Brittany. However, they can also be heard at midnight near lonely streams outside villages and towns. Should any traveller come upon them, he is forced to help them wring the sheets in the same direction – if he does not, he will be thrown into the water and drowned. If he succeeds, the washerwomen are released from their task.

In Scotland and Ireland it is the *bean nighe*, described as washing in lonely streams the bloodstained clothes of those who are about to die. *Bean* means woman and *nighe* night. One legend says that they are women who died in childbirth and will continue to wash clothes until the day they would have died of natural causes. This reflects the taboos surrounding childbirth, which in earlier times could be dangerous. It was regarded as a magical period when the dimensions parted to allow the new soul to enter, and so might attract all kinds of fearsome creatures. Those who see the washerwomen, especially at a ford, would know that a major change was going to take place in their lives. If one can get between the washerwomen and the water without being seen first, they are compelled to grant three wishes.

Bean sidhe

The most prevalent image of the banshee or 'woman of the fairy', a literal translation of *bean sidhe*, in Ireland and

Scotland was in one of the three aspects associated with the Triple Goddess from whom she is descended: a lovely maiden, a mature woman or a hag. Also called the White Lady of Sorrows, she is depicted in all her forms wearing a grey, hooded cloak or a ragged veil with eyes red from weeping. Chapter 3 described how in Scotland and America she was sometimes seen on a white horse.

Her special wail heralding a death, called a keening, has been described as quite musical and immensely comforting, especially if a person has been ill and in pain or is very old and is fading away. Some beautiful Irish funeral music is based, it is claimed, on the songs of the banshee, who will be heard singing at the funeral as she guides her beloved mortal kin to the Otherworld.

Like other hags, the banshee can appear as a hooded crow, a stoat, a hare or a weasel. All these creatures are considered unlucky near a sick room, and the last of them at any time by Romany gypsies.

In Cornwall a banshee is seen outside the window of a dying person flapping her cloak. For this reason she is some-times mistaken for a crow or owl, both birds of misfortune and heralds of death.

FAIRY GODDESSES/QUEENS

The fairy goddesses and queens are the maiden or mother aspects of goddess worship. They are invariably beautiful, but were also sometimes war-like and symbols of power, rather than the ethereal but relatively tame Titania in Shakespeare's *A Midsummer Night's Dream*. However, Titania herself may link with the fierce Greek Titan gods and goddesses.

Aine

Daughter of Manannan, Lord of the Isle of Man, Aine seems to have retained her full power in the persona of the fairy queen of Munster in Ireland. She is linked with love, fertility, healing and the cycles of the solar and lunar year. Her worship was recalled even in the twentieth century on the Hill of Aine by torchlight processions and burning straw at midsummer, and also at the old corn harvest, Lughnassadh, at the beginning of August.

Aine had human lovers by whom she bore many children, creating a special fairy race. Eventually she agreed to marry Gerald, the Earl of Desmond, who stole her magical cloak and so gained power over her. They had a child who was known as the Magician because of his wonderful powers. Aine warned Gerald that he must never express amazement at the young man's deeds, or he would lose his power over her and the child. But when his son leaped in and out of a bottle the Earl was unable to keep silent, the spell was broken and Aine was able to return to the fairies.

The date given for this event by folklorists was 1398. At this time her son too flew away in the form of a goose, to live beneath Lough Fur in County Limerick. Every seven years he emerges to ride around the edge of the lake on his magical white horse with silver shoes, and it is said he will do so until the shoes wear out. It is at this time that the lough appears briefly as dry land and a tree grows from beneath the lake, covered by a green cloth. Beneath the tree, the lake guardian can be seen knitting. Under the lake is an entrance to Tir na n'Og, the Celtic Otherworld.

Cliodna

Another daughter of Manannan, Cliodna of the Golden Hair, rules over the sea and the afterlife and is Queen of the Land of Promise, a realm of the Otherworld in which there is always peace and harmony. Every ninth wave is sacred to her, and if wishes are placed in shells, tied with seaweed and cast on the ninth wave to reach the shore she will grant them. She heals the sick with her magical birds.

Repeated to be the most beautiful woman in the world in mortal form, she took mortal lovers to Fairyland. None of them returned except for Ciabhan, whom Cliodna loved so much that she left the Otherworld to live with him. However, while he was hunting her father Manannan sent a fairy minstrel to enchant her as she slept on the shore and carried her back to Fairyland in a magical sleep. She is seen on seashores, either as a huge wave or a seabird, calling for her lost love.

FAIRY WOMEN AND THE PATRIARCHY

The Morgans or Morgana

The alter ego of the mermaids are the Morgana. In Brittany there is a whole tradition of powerful sea fairy goddesses who cause storms and drag sailors to their deaths beneath the waves in an unsuccessful attempt to satisfy their own passions.

The Morgana legends first appeared in the sixth century at the time Brittany was Christianised, when the powerful Druidesses and noblewomen would not submit to the patriarchal power of the Church. The first Morgan was Dahut, daughter of Gradlon, King of Cornouaille in Brittany, who built Ys, a beautiful city below sea level with walls to keep back the water. A dyke was opened to allow the citizens to carry out their craft of fishing.

Dahut still worshipped the old gods and so was in constant conflict with Corentin, the bishop of Quimper. She was accused of bringing disrepute to the city with her unbridled passions and, it is claimed, caused the destruction of the city by handing the keys of the dyke, which she had stolen from her father, to a new lover, identified in legend as the Devil. He opened the dyke and the sea drowned all the inhabitants except for Gradlon and the bishop. Dahut clung to the back of her father's horse, but the bishop told Gradlon to cast her into the sea or he too would be drowned. So the fond father pushed his daughter into the sea, leaving her to perish.

Dahut did not die but was transformed into the vengeful sea goddess Marie Morgan, who drags sailors to their doom. In this form she interrupted a mass to save the souls of those drowned in Ys. It is said that because of this the inhabitants still live in their city under the sea, trapped until Judgement Day.

Fishermen at nearby Douarnenez still hear the bells ring under the sea. When I visited the town in May it was shrouded in mist like the entire Finisterre coast and, except for a shop selling *santons*, tiny clay Nativity figures, seemed as though it held many secrets.

So Dahut became Morgan, the prototype of the vengeful sea women of Brittany. There were sea women before Dahut, of course, but she gave them a cloak of identity.

It could be argued that Dahut, who stood for the Old Religion, was unfairly demonised and that her father sacrificed her to save his own position. The same happened to Sedna, the sea woman of the Inuit who live beyond the Arctic Circle. Once a lovely maiden, she is now a sea hag who holds the fertility of the fish and seals under her command, but can be vengeful. While she and her father, Angusta, were being pursued by her demon lover Kokksaut in the form of a sea bird, her father pushed her out of their canoe, then chopped off her fingers so that she could not cling on.

I feel that the anger of the sea women who can never be satisfied reflects a whole culture of female power that was buried under the sea. However, the power is not lost and feminist psychotherapists use such myths as a focus for women's exploration of their innate fierce survival instincts.

The Morgan is portrayed rising to the surface with her women when the sun glints on the sea, and in the moonlight, sitting on a rock, she combs her hair with a golden comb. Sedna, rather more raddled, demands that shamans comb her tangled locks before she will release her bounty to the fishermen.

FAIRY GODS/KINGS

Ankou

Finvarra, King of the Western Fairies and of Death, has already appeared in this book. But an even more enigmatic and powerful figure in Brittany is Ankou, the Fairy Lord, once deity of Death. His role is to collect the souls of those who have recently died. He is described as wearing black and covering his face, for it is said that no living person can look on him. Ankou drives a black cart, or in more upmarket legend a black carriage pulled by four black horses; this ghostly carriage features in the folk legends of many lands. Music may herald his arrival, and in my own research I have come across stories of people living in the wilds of Ireland who suddenly hear the music of a wake just before someone dies, even though the nearest house is miles away. The sound of the carriage and Ankou's knock at the door would coincide with a death in the house.

Ankou was said to have his own paths in Brittany along which he and the dead passed in procession on what is now Halloween. As in modern Mexico, people would prepare feasts to be left by the hearth for departed relations. In the early part of the twentieth century, in Breton custom milk was poured on graves as libations on 1 November, All Saints' Day, and each village regarded as its annual Ankou the last adult to die during the previous year.

The Erl King

The Erl or Elf King was featured in song and story long before written accounts. Associated with the Black Forest in Germany, where he is called the *Erlkönig*, he is also known as *Ellerkonge* in Denmark. Made famous by Goethe's poem written in 1782, which was translated by several writers including Sir Walter Scott, the Erl King was notorious for abducting children and appeared to warn people of their impending death and its manner. The two may be closely linked in times of high child mortality and, as with similar abductions by supernatural forces, it can be argued that he helped parents to overcome their own guilt at a child's death that they could not prevent by blaming a powerful force beyond their control.

In 1815 the Austrian composer Franz Schubert set Goethe's poem to music. The poem tells of a child riding through a snowstorm who tells his father he can see the Elf King. Since only a person about to die sees the King, the father dismisses the child's words as imagination and says it is only the leaves rustling. However, he becomes afraid when the child says the Elf King has hurt him and rides for home as fast as he can. But by the time father and son reach the courtyard of the house the child is dead.

In a version translated by Edwin Zeydel in 1955, the Erl King asks the boy:

> *Sweet lad, o come and join me, do!*
> *Such pretty games I will play with you;*
> *On the shore gay flowers their colour unfold,*
> *My mother has many garments of gold.*
>
> *Will you, sweet lad, come along with me?*
> *My daughters shall care for you tenderly;*
> *In the night my daughters their revelry keep,*
> *They'll rock you and dance you and sing you to sleep.*

Such characters as Ankou and the Erl King have slipped back into fairy tale and the Grim Reaper, a similar form in England, has become a joke figure. Death itself has become taboo – the stuff of either comedy or horror films. In ordinary life, many like to believe it no longer has a place.

Manannan Mac Lir

One of the most powerful fairy lords was Manannan Mac Lir, or Manannan-Beg-Mac-y-Leir in Manx fairy lore.

Originally a sea deity of Ireland, he was said to be the foster-father of Lugh, young God of Light. He was Lord of the Isles of the Blest, which, as well as the Isle of Man, included the Isle of Arran on which the magic cauldron of Annwyn was kept. Because of this Manannan was a guardian of the Grail treasures. He is still special protector of the Isle of Man, which is named after him.

Though he is most often pictured in a green robe with a golden circlet round his head, Manannan is an expert shape-shifter; indeed, he seduced many mortal women on nocturnal visits in the form of a heron or sea bird. His fairy palace was on the Isle of Arran, known as Emhain of the Apple Trees, a connection with the Otherworld Isle of Avalon, the Isle of Apples. He was said in some legends to have ferried the dying Arthur and Merlin to the Otherworld. Manannan's magic pigs, which were constantly reborn once they were killed, were used by the Tuatha de Danaan and later the *daoine sidhe*, the fairy court, to keep them eternally young, because the swine themselves ate windfall apples from the magical trees of youth.

In his fairy form he was regarded as a master magician who, to protect the Isle of Man, would either cast down a mist from his great mountain or float pea shells with sticks for masts and cast glamour round them. Any enemies would be driven away by the sight of such a mighty fleet. His magical armour meant that he could never be wounded, and it was his powers that helped the Tuatha become invisible when they were forced underground by the Milesian invasion. Indeed, Manannan was said to have caused the separation of the world of mortals and the world of fairies by shaking his cloak between his wife Fand and her lover Cuchulainn, the hero son of Lugh, who had lived in Fairyland with her for a month, so that they might never be together again in the same dimension.

EXERCISE: RAISING THE POWER OF THE FAIRIES OF FATE

Many of the goddesses and fairies of fate are associated in legend with pools of destiny. For example, The Well of Wyrd or Fate at the foot of the World Tree was guarded by the Viking Norns. In this well, each morning the Norns read the destiny of the gods.

These pools of destiny were older even than the crystal ball for scrying – seeing images in the water. In the case of pools that were traditionally close to a World Tree, patterns were cast by the branches and leaves in the water. That water came from the original Well of Wisdom in the Otherworld, whose entrance is at Connla in Ireland.

If you have a question to ask you can create a pool of fate. Remember that this fate is not fixed but a combination of what has been, what is and the path you will take, which will be influenced by the as yet unknown opportunities or challenges that await you.

There are three methods to choose from, and the images formed in your mind's eye that are triggered by the water can be interpreted by using the same personal image system that helps you to understand your dreams (I have written more about this in *The Complete Guide to Psychic Development*). These symbolic meanings are those we gained from fairy stories as children, from what we read and from personal experiences, as well as knowledge we access through our genes and our psyche from the collective pool of knowledge.

The sunlight method

- Take a clear crystal or glass bowl and half-fill it with water.

- Place it where the sun shines directly into it.

- Take a fern or small leafy branch and wave it over the surface, so that it creates moving shadows on the water.

- As you do so, focus on a question about an opportunity or a problem you need to overcome. Alternatively, allow your mind to go blank and let your unconscious direct you as to the meaning of what you will see.

- If you cannot immediately see an image, close your eyes, open them, blink, look at the water and say the first word or phrase that comes into your head, however unlikely. In adulthood we are so accustomed to working in words that the spontaneous image system of childhood that grants direct access to the psychic may take longer to reactivate.

- Continue until you have two or three images.

The moonlight method

- Fill your bowl, but this time take it out under a bright full or nearly full moon, so that the bowl is filled with silver light.

- This time, ripple the surface three separate times with a crystal pendulum or gently drop tiny crystals or glass nuggets into the bowl, one after the other, to gain your three images.

The candlelight method

- Colour your water with dark ink or the traditional mugwort infusion (its fragrance was said to induce psychic visions).

- Either surround your bowl with tall white candles so that they cast light into the water, or use floating candles in white or yellow that you can gently push to create moving images.

- Make the rest of the room dark and again wait until you have three images, rippling the water as necessary.

- A light breeze can help the candles to create moving patterns of light and shadow.

Note your symbols and the meanings you assign them in your fairy book. As you use this method on other occasions you can add to the list. If a meaning eludes you, weave the three pictures into a story and retell it just before you fall asleep.

After a few months, many people find that their own symbolic meanings do bear striking similarities to those given in books on scrying or tea leaf reading. If this happens to you, you will know that you are accessing the universal archetypes that underpin all ages and cultures.

CHAPTER TEN

Fairies and the Arthurian Tradition

Only reapers, reaping early
In among the bearded barley,

Hear a song that echoes cheerly
Down the river winding clearly,
Down to tower'd Camelot:
And by the moon the reaper weary,
Piling sheaves in uplands airy,
Listening, whispers ''Tis the fairy
Lady of Shalott.'

'The Lady of Shalott', ALFRED LORD TENNYSON
(1809–1892)

airy traditions are interwoven throughout the Arthurian legends. In the earlier versions the Lady of the Lake is a fairy. However, as the stories were made more sophisticated and the courtly aspects became more prominent, fairies become enchantresses and the knights relied on earthly courage and prayer rather than supernatural powers to slay dragons and rescue fair damsels.

Nevertheless the otherworldly aspects never entirely fade. I have followed only a few of the more important fairy themes, but on p. 243–245 have suggested books that you can read on the subject of Arthur and the Grail. The Arthur/ Merlin/Lady of the Lake symbols have been reworked many times in different ages and cultures. One of the best modern versions is Marion Zimmer Bradley's *Mists of Avalon*, which recounts events from the feminist perspective through Morgan le Fey, Arthur's half-sister.

THE LADY OF THE LAKE

In Welsh, Cornish and Breton folklore the Arthurian Lady of the Lake is a synthesis of myriad lake, river and water spirits that are a feature of the green lands inhabited by the Celts. One of the most important roles of the Arthurian Lady of the Lake is as guardian of the sacred sword Excalibur. This was one of the thirteen sacred Celtic treasures, the sword of Nuada of the Silver Hand whose sword hand was cut off in battle. With a new hand fashioned of silver he went on to lead his people to victory.

Associated also with Lugh, the hero who became the young Celtic Sun God, it was one of the treasures of the Dagda, the Father God. In its Christianised form, the sword was identified with that of King David.

The magical sword was given to Arthur as hero king who dedicated himself to the defence of the land. Mythologically he was a reincarnated solar deity and his Round Table was a gigantic Sun Wheel. Morgan le Fey wove him an enchanted scabbard that would protect him from serious injury in battle while he possessed it, but later took back this gift in an action sometimes seen as spite. However, in her role as touchstone of the sacred duty of kingship she felt that he was betraying the old way of worship.

In some versions the Lady of the Lake was a fairy woman. But in an older tradition she was one of the ancient goddesses of life, death and rebirth.

Various names are given to the supreme Lady of the Lake, depending on the particular tradition. Because the Arthurian legends span many generations, the persona of the Lake Lady changes. But she is always an archetypal Moon Goddess/Queen to Arthur's Sun King. Indeed, it has been said that the queens of Avalon were of a far older lineage than Arthur's, and so he was spiritually and emotionally a liege to them. The most significant are Nimue or Nineve, and in Brittany Viviane or Vivien, an enchantress of fairy stock and, some say, like Morgan le Fey a high priestess of Avalon, a realm of the Otherworld. In some accounts Vivien is aunt of Morgan le Fey, and King Arthur and Morgan or Nimue become her successor.

Although Vivien's lake is identified in the enchanted Breton forest of Brociliande near Rennes, another Arthurian legend describes Merlin riding with Arthur into Dozmary Pool on Bodmin Moor in Cornwall. Here he pulled Excalibur from a floating stone to which after his death Sir Bedivere returned it, and here the hand of the Lake Lady took it beneath the waters.

The Lady of the Lake was also said to be the foster-mother or even the actual mother of Sir Lancelot, one of Arthur's knights, after the Great Rite in which his father, the Breton King Bran, made a sacred marriage with the Earth and so with one of the ancient priestesses of the goddess, possibly the Lake Lady or High Priestess herself. Lancelot was in some tales orphaned and taken by the fairy lady to her island and, because he was brought up in the land of fairy, became half-fey, if it was not already in his blood. According to Sir Thomas Malory in his poem *Morte d'Arthur*, written in 1485, Lancelot's fairy wife/lover Elaine/Elayne was expelled from the kingdom by the jealous Gwenhwyvar or Guinevere. Elaine nursed Lancelot in the land of fairy from a near-fatal wound caused by a boar before sending him back to Arthur's court and Guinevere.

THE LADIES OF THE LAKE

Confusion may arise partly because some traditions talk of nine Ladies of the Lake. In earlier legends of the original

Grail or Graal it was not a cup, but the magic cauldron of Annwyn. Its guardians were nine maidens, according to the tales of the sixth-century bard Taliesin, himself sometimes regarded as a reincarnation of Merlin. The nine maidens were believed to live on an island of priestesses in the middle of a lake or across the seas – a link perhaps with the ancient colleges of Druidesses or with the Celtic Otherworld island, the Land of Women. The Celtic experts and authors of many books on the subject, John and Caitlin Matthews, developed the concept of the nine lake women as a secret sisterhood, each of whom embodied different characteristics of the Sacred Feminine that lies at the heart of the Arthurian mysteries. The imagery of the Lake Ladies may reflect the female/goddess form of the patriarchal Knights of the Round Table, and in many stories the lake is regarded as an illusion to protect the magical world from those who cannot accept the magic.

According to the writings of the twelfth-century bishop of St Asaph, Geoffrey of Monmouth, Ynis Avallah, the Isle of Apples or Avalon, was ruled by nine sisters, the chief of which was the enchantress Morgan le Fey. Avalon was frequently associated with the spiritual or magical isle of Glastonbury.

The Ladies of the Lake, sometimes called the nine Fairy Queens, who travelled with Arthur on his funeral barge included Arthur's mother Igraine – herself of fairy blood and who conceived Arthur by Uther Pendragon under enchantment – and Arthur's fey wife Gwenhwyvar/Guinevere. These women were bonded not by liking, indeed in the Arthurian legends, there was loathing between Morgan and Arthur's wife. But in a mystical sense, each of the women served a role in the life and death of Arthur, reuniting on his funeral barge. So they were joined through him, like points of a web at which he was at the centre.

MORGAN LE FEY

This character probably provokes more controversy than any other in Arthurian legend. The more Christian the legend the more problematic her fey connections, and the more the evil witch persona takes over from the priestess of the Old Religion/Queen of the Fairies.

Morgan the Fairy has been described as the half-sister of King Arthur or his cousin and in many of the older myths was the mother of Mordred – conceived, it is sometimes said, from her union with Arthur in the Sacred Marriage, the symbolic sacred sex rite with the Earth, as a priestess when neither was aware of the identity of the other. In ancient dynasties, union between close kin was a way of ensuring that the blood line was not diluted.

Some traditions see her as a form of the Celtic Mother Goddess, Matrona, Morgen, a goddess associated with winter and death, or, like the Breton Morgana, a vengeful creature of the sea. The word 'fey' is linked with both fairy and fate, and she has also been associated with the Irish triple goddesses the Morrighu who traditionally protected hero kings.

She was, however, said to be intent on Arthur's destruction because, in the way of fairies, she was jealous to see him with his wife. But I prefer the explanation that she was the guardian of his sacred kingship and was angry when Arthur proved less than worthy in his later years, listening to priests rather than to Merlin and allowing the power of the Solar Wheel (the Round Table) to be dissipated by the obsession with the Grail Quest. As a result of the Knights going their separate paths, and some dying and others going insane, those who sought the Grail to bring healing to the land left the realm vulnerable to the treachery of Mordred, one of their own company. However, some believe Morgan's malice was because Arthur's father had killed her own father, Gorlois, the Duke of Cornwall.

Indeed, the Christianised Grail cup floating through the air at Pentecost over the Round Table, in some tales carried by an ethereal Grail maiden guardian, was as magical as it was religious. The Church remained ambivalent about the Grail literature, because it was imbued with occult as well as mystical significance.

ARTHUR AS A FAIRY KING

The original historical Arthur was an ancient British king of Celtic origin who, in the fifth century, united parts of Britain against hostile invading forces after the collapse of the Roman Empire and the return home of the occupying

Romans. In AD 496, under the command of Arthur, the Britons defeated the Saxons at the siege of Mount Badon, the last of twelve battles according to the monk Nennius, writing in 800, which resulted in a generation of peace. Arthur is said to have slain 960 men single-handed at Badon.

However, he is also linked with an earlier Welsh god of the same name. In medieval times the legend of the Christianised Grail or sacred chalice became the focus of the Arthurian legends, but in reality it was only one part. The Knights became transformed from being akin to the Irish Fianna, the magical warriors of the hero King Fionn, to represent the idealistic, courtly values of the Middle Ages rather than those of the historical King Arthur.

Arthur's fey links come through his mother Igraine, and he was guided by Merlin the magician, the son of an Underworld King or spirit and a mortal mother. Merlin was said to reincarnate in many lifetimes when his powers were needed. In one or two versions Merlin too is the son of Uther Pendragon, and after his death, Merlin became in some legends, Lord of the Underworld, thus making him a kind of spiritual Arthur.

ARTHUR IN THE OTHERWORLD

An early Welsh poem, 'Preiddeu Annwyn', tells how Arthur sailed to Annwyn with his companions and stole from Caer Sidi, the Fortress of the Fairies, the cauldron that would heal the sick and wounded, feed the hungry at Arthur's table and protect them from plague and ageing. It was also the cauldron of prophecy. In a later, Christianised, version Arthur stole the cauldron from demons and kept it on Mount Snowdon. Either way, in Arthurian hero terms he went to the Otherworld in a shamanic quest to bring healing and knowledge of magic into the world where it might bring fertility and abundance to the land.

When Arthur was slain by his son Mordred, he returned to the Isle of Avalon to be healed by the Mother Goddess until he is needed to return. The old god was struck down by the new and younger deity, but because Arthur was a magical being and the fight involved treachery Mordred too died of a wound received from Arthur.

THE FAIRY BRIDE

Gwenhwyvar or Guinevere, Arthur's queen, is also regarded as having fairy blood. Unlike the dark-haired tiny Morgan, the golden-haired Guinevere, whose name means 'white fairy', or 'white phantom', was said to be one of the Tylwyth Teg, the Fairy Folk of Wales. In the Malory poem Melwas or Meligaunt, who abducted Gwenhwyvar, has been linked with Midir, a king of the Tuatha de Danaan who was eternally young. She was rescued from her abduction and seduction by the fey Lancelot. Some say she was imprisoned in the hollow hill on Glastonbury Tor and so her abductor was sometimes regarded as Gwynn ap Nudd, the guardian of the Tor, known in this role as the Dark Arthur.

The fairy link is confirmed in the Malory version of events, among other sources. Guinevere ordered her court to dress in green, the fairy colour, and 'go a maying', the fairy festival at which she was abducted.

MERLIN

Merlin is best known as the wizard/counsellor who watched over Arthur from before his birth and helped him to fulfil his destiny. His character was based on a sixth-century North Wales bard called Myrddin who seems to have lived through at least three kings' reigns, of which Arthur's was the last, though Geoffrey of Monmouth associated him only with Uther Pendragon, Arthur's father. His magic was at odds with the Christianised medieval courtly emphasis and so he left several times to wander in Brittany/the Otherworld.

Indeed, the most compelling tales of Merlin are of his sojourns in Brittany where he fell in love with Nimue/Vivien. Merlin created for her a palace beneath the Lake and taught her his magical arts to add to her own. She used this magic to enclose Merlin in a tower/cave/tomb/enchanted wood/nine magic rings from which he could not escape, so that he would never leave her. Others say he lives in the land of fairy, waiting for the call for the return of

Arthur and guarding the sacred treasures of the Celts. The tower was occasionally described as glass, linking with the glass palace of Caer Wydyr in Annwyn and one of the names for Glastonbury, Ynis Witrin, the Island of Glass.

In a poem written by the American Edward Arlington Robinson (1869–1935), Merlin loves Vivien so much that he willingly allows himself to be bound by her. This legend is filled with possibilities of a far deeper meaning – it makes no sense that a master magician would unknowingly create the means of his own destruction. Was the love affair a struggle between the patriarchy and the old Mother Goddess religions, resolved in the ultimate union in which Merlin chose to become eternally bound to Nimue/Vivien in Fairyland? Or had Merlin, in his role of Archdruid, offended against some ancient law by allowing his power to be corrupted, whether for love or for political ends? Was his desertion of Arthur the Sun King at his time of need, for the love of the Lake Lady, regarded as an abuse of his magic, especially if Arthur was his brother? Did Merlin suffer the ancient rite in which a Druid said to have committed treason against the Order was enclosed alive in an oak tree? Was his earthly time drawing to a close and so he retired to Avalon and the Lake Lady to die?

In the Forest of Brociliande near Rennes is a spot known as the tomb of Merlin, a Neolithic tomb overhung with trees on which wishes and petitions, babies' booties, ribbons and wreaths of wild flowers have been placed. Coins are also pushed into the slots, bearing such messages as 'In these hard times, Merlin, help me to get a job' and 'thanks for blessings received.' Clearly the place has acquired spiritual significance over the years as people have gone there with hopes and wishes.

The forest is totally unspoilt and the tomb scarcely marked. I found it significant on my recent visit there that the spirituality of the place was far greater than many conventional religious shrines I have visited. Three months later at least part of my own wish to Merlin seemed to be coming to fruition.

Though some archaeologists are convinced that Glastonbury was not the seat of Avalon and that Arthur's stronghold was near Shrewsbury, few can doubt the Otherworldly associations of Glastonbury in spite of the incredible commercialisation of recent years. It is the only place I have been where it is not only possible but probable to slip spontaneously into fairy time. Perhaps the most dramatic example was when I and my very sceptical husband visited the White Springs next to the Chalice Well. We were unable to park near by and so left the car at the top of a hill some fifteen minutes' walk away. We arrived at the springs hot and irritable. Yet sitting in the cave through which the spring runs (a café has been installed there but has destroyed none of the mystery), it is hard not to be lulled by the magic, and we began the return journey up the very steep hill in a more optimistic mood. We started up the first section of road, turned the corner and there was the car – less than five minutes uphill from the cave. We could not believe it. I have no explanation for the time discrepancy, except that we moved into fairy time. Even my husband was silenced.

WHAT DOES IT ALL MEAN?

So many versions, so many avenues of mystery and magic. Any man, woman or child can create their own version of the Arthurian legend, given the basic characters, and create a valid account. I suppose my own conclusion would be that there are three levels and three pairings. Nimue/Vivien and Merlin represented the High Priest and Priestess, figures who are central to magic and who ritually re-enact the Sacred Marriage of Goddess and God, thus ensuring the fertility of the land. The second pairing between Morgan le Fey as Priestess of the Old Religion and Arthur as Christian King symbolically represented the union of the spiritual power of the Mother goddess with the earthly power of the sovereign. As descendants of the fairies Lancelot and Guinevere symbolised the coupling of fairy king and fairy queen. Thus the legends of Arthur contain quite profound magical depths.

EXERCISE: STEPPING INTO THE LEGENDS

- Wait until after dusk during the period of the waning moon when the inner world is more powerful than the outer.

- Light a yellow or cream beeswax candle and allow the gentle honeyed fragrance within the world of the candle flame to unfold.

- Breathe in gently and slowly the golden light, and exhale darkness until the light surrounds you and you can see or visualise quite clearly a doorway in it.

- Step in your mind's vision through the doorway into an enchanted forest where the flowers are brighter, the trees more green and small animals and birds approach without fear.

- Ahead you can see a castle and within the courtyard a golden-haired king in armour and a pale-haired queen surrounded by knights and fairy maidens.

- Watch the pageantry and see how the king emits a halo of gold, for this is a Sun hero. The queen is a representative of the White Goddess, a moon maiden, and surrounding her is an aura of pure silver. The king and queen may speak to you and offer wise words or encouragement, suggesting practical steps or new avenues you can take towards achieving your dreams.

- Move on, climbing turret stairs to a dark room like an alchemist's laboratory in which a wizard is working, making phials of jewelled potions. He will not give you a direct message, but produce magical symbols from his cauldron that you can interpret at a later time.

- Go out once more and meet a tiny elfin woman in a dark robe, who will take you to the shores of a lake where a barge is waiting.

- Through the mist you may see a palace of glass or a grove of trees with standing stones in which priestesses, perhaps the nine lake maidens, and Druids are performing ancient rituals.

- When you reach the island, your guide may show you herbs and crystals and give you the names of those that will help and strengthen you.

- Finally you will meet the Lady of the Lake, who appears differently to everyone who approaches her in dreams or visions. She may have a magic mirror or a clear crystal in which she will allow you to gaze, or she may wordlessly impart some secret that will be of guidance when you return to the world.

- Retrace your route through the doorway of light.

- Sit in the candlelight and let the scenes develop in your psyche. Words spoken in the experience expand as inner dialogue, and the magical rituals and their relevance to your life become clear.

- Note the symbols that were offered from the cauldron and the herbs and crystals that the elfin woman showed you.

- When the candle is burned through, sleep and let your dreams weave patterns around your candle vision.

- The next day try to buy or find the herbs and crystals, if you do not already possess them, and learn more of their uses. On p. 243 I have suggested books that may help.

- Finally begin your own story, painting or a poem of fairy queens, knights, magicians and ladies of the lake, based on the pictures you saw in the candle flame. When you reread it you may be surprised at the insights it holds into your own life and future.

Where Are the Fairies?

Two fairies it was
On a still summer day
Came forth in the woods
With the flowers to play.

'Spoils of the Dead', ROBERT FROST (1874–1963)

While I have been writing this book, I have experienced wonderful dreams of enchanted woodlands, fairies dancing in rings to the sound of pipes made from elder trees, nature spirits of tree and waterfall, and the magical creatures whose presence can be felt in places where earth energies are at their most powerful.

The Isle of Wight, where I live, is a place in which everything is in miniature – rolling downs, low cliffs, copses and groves of trees, small thatched villages – and nowhere is more than 15 miles (25 kilometres) from the sea. It is real fairy country, and when the mist rolls in across the downs or the marshes it could be Avalon.

But fairies are not confined to particular places, though it may be easier to tune into them in unspoilt countryside; nor are they merely pretty, dainty, winged creatures that flit around flowers. They are also symbols of power and transformation. The ugly hag is possessed of the same magic and maybe more wisdom than the golden-haired lake maidens. The dwarves mining underground, the brownie working in the barn and the trolls hiding behind trees in the uncharted forests of Scandinavia are the other end of the spectrum from the stately kings and queens and their fairy courts under the green hillside or the mermaids singing mesmerically, and are just as important. Fairies of all kinds are part of the folk memory we carry within us, passed down over the millennia in our genes and in song and story.

Rather than fairies disappearing, it may be we who have moved away, too often living and working in crowded towns with concrete squares and neatly trimmed greenery. The earth, rather than remaining as it has been for millennia the home of a myriad creatures in overlapping dimensions, has become a larder and fuel source for humans, to be raided at any time without worry of replenishment. Nature is out there, the cold is excluded by central heating, the darkness by constant electric light. Food is available even out of season in the supermarket to those with the money to buy it, and travel is no longer an encounter with nature at its most glorious and fearsome but dulled by constant chatter on mobile phones, in-flight movies and motel chains that are standardised from Hong Kong to Greenland.

Times and Places to see Fairies, According to Different Traditions
Children and psychics can see fairies at any time and in any
place. But for most mortals Midsummer Eve at dusk, especially
if the moon is full, is the best fey time of all. Each twenty-
four-hour period has transition times at sunrise, noon, sunset
and midnight. At these times doorways may be seen between
the world of fey and mortals.

The old agricultural festivals are also occasions when fairy
activity heightens and they may be more readily visible. Leave
some of the harvest feast at the Autumn Equinox for the fairies
and it is believed you will lack nothing materially in the coming
year.

May Eve (30 April), like Midsummer Eve, is an occasion
when fairy revels are most joyous and human contact is not
shunned. Travellers passing single standing stones have seen a
lighted doorway in the stone and heard the sounds of music and
feasting from within.

However, on Samhain, the predecessor of Halloween, fairies
are less friendly and malevolent spirits such as goblins take
advantage of the parting of the barriers between past, present
and future to make mischief. Place a Jack o' lantern at your
window and food on the hearth for friendly fairies. If you are
brave enough, go to a crossroads where the wind will tell you
what the future holds. Divination at Halloween especially for
love has been practised through the ages – look in the mirror at
midnight as you comb your hair and you will see, courtesy of
the old magic, your future or present love, and you will dream
of golden tomorrows.

Does it matter when we can stimulate almost any experience
with technological wizardry, our very own fairy glamour;
when science can explain, categorise and provide artificial

forms of almost any natural substance; when psychiatry can alleviate sadness and fears and increase joy with a tablet or behaviour modification? We have our own mortal fairies in the models or pop stars who marry handsome young foot-ballers, the nuptials recorded for all to share in the modern equivalent of the fairy tale, society magazines. When the media fairy princesses are no longer young and lovely or get divorced, there are new ethereal icons about whom to weave myths of happy ever afters.

But perhaps we are waking from this plastic fairyland after what seems a hundred-year sleep to find our forests devas-tated, our seas polluted, increasing numbers of children asthmatic or hyperactive, their imaginations stunted by simu-lated cartoon worlds and video games in which they can zap the goblins and gremlins but never talk to the elves or watch the pixies. The happy pills have side-effects, modified foods may damage our health and all the New Age workshops in the world cannot substitute for the magic and mystery of the natural world and its creatures. The butterfly is a miracle of aerodynamics – it is also beautiful and ethereal and may well be a sylph in disguise. When we seek to contact extra-terrestrial beings, we are also reawakening those that exist within our own world. Maybe they are one and the same.

When we reclaim herb and crystal lore, reread and retell the old legends and fairy lore, we are re-establishing that connection to our innate spiritual nature and to the fey within us all. That is the part that uses glamour not to deceive but to illuminate the mundane and reveal possibilities within the most unpromising place and situation. It is the power that does not turn away from hags or fear giants, but uses their inherent strength and transformative powers to face and change reality. Wishing on stars, rainbows or at the tomb of Merlin are not the pleas of the unenlightened, but are based in a deep instinctual awareness that there are natural energies that can be harnessed to turn endeavour into success, hope into despair.

You may never see a fairy with your physical eyes. On the other hand you may, and of course it will be such a privilege, such a precious moment that you may want to keep it a secret. Our ancestors who encountered fairy folk on hill-sides, in woods and in their homes did not demand objective proof. Rather, they welcomed such encounters and shared them in evenings by the fireside with friends, neighbours and children, so passing on a special and quite sacred heritage. At the same time they feared the unknown and intangible, for to come face to face with another dimension does destroy many things we hold as certainties, provoking questions about our own nature and that of the universe. We cannot dismiss what we cannot see with our physical eyes any more than we can ignore the possibility of life in other galaxies, because we have only what sceptics call anecdotal evidence but sensitives call a wealth of human experience.

Fairies are part of our heritage and a legacy we leave to our children. Whether they are a psychic or symbolic phenomenon or another race of beings on a different vibration from our own, we owe it to future generations to keep alive the lore that is both unique to each land and yet possesses a common core and symbolism. Magic is all around us, not in fairy gold or escapes to lands where time stands still and every day is a festival. It resides in the ability to enjoy moments of happiness out of time, to see the wonders of a world we did not create and do not know who did. It is to realise that life is far more unpredictable, wilder and so much more exciting than we ever imagined, even as children. Above all, maybe wishes can come true. So make one, and enjoy the anticipation.

An A–Z of
World Fairies

This section includes brief references to fairies described within the main chapters, as well as others in more detail from different traditions around the world. I have distinguished between male and female forms where their roles differ or one sex predominates in sightings and legends.

Each kind of fairy is in a sense like the description of a Tarot card; for though each type does have specific characteristics, seeing fairy folk is subjective. You can write any fey names that seem relevant to you in your journal and allow your psyche to weave a story or an image that you can paint or draw. There are countless sites on the World Wide Web with free fairy pictures to download, some of paintings that are quite beautiful, or you might collect cards or fairy books or figurines. I have listed a few companies in the Useful Addresses on p. 246 from which you can obtain catalogues, but you should check out different sources both on the Web and in directories as there is a wealth of fairy collectables from the truly inspired to the frankly tacky.

Abatwa

Very small, shy southern African fairies who live in anthills. They are only seen by young children and pregnant women, perhaps because these are particularly fey conditions in mortals.

Ballybog

Small brown Irish fairy of the peat bogs, known as bogles in Cornwall and Wales where they inhabit boggy land. They are appeased with offerings to allow peat to be cut for fuel, and numerous coins etc. have been discovered preserved in peat bogs (some, of course, just dropped accidentally). However, it is known that ritual sacrifice of humans was made in peat bogs, so the original bog spirits may have been very powerful Earth deities (now diminished in size and power).

Bean fionn

The Irish form of a water woman also found in German and English folklore. The Irish white-robed *bean fionn* is said to drag children and travellers beneath the water. The English Jenny Greenteeth is found in Yorkshire; in the form of a lovely maiden she seduces young males and then drags them beneath the water in her hag form, with sagging breasts, a distended stomach and green teeth. In Germany, however, the *Weisse Frau* will guard children and travellers, drowning only those who harm children.

Bean nighe
The Scottish version of the banshee, herald of death, to be found washing bloodstained shrouds in streams. It is a term also for the phantom washerwomen of Ireland who wash bloodstained clothes. In Brittany they are the *lavandières*.

Bean sidhe
The Irish banshee, the female who wails before the death of members of certain ancient aristocratic Irish families. If the sound of several banshees is heard simultaneously, the soul of a great or holy person is passing over.

Bean tighe
An Irish fairy housekeeper/godmother who cares for mothers, children and pets and will finish chores around the home. Like the banshee, she may be attached to a family for generations.

Blue men of the Minch
Blue sea creatures living round the Scottish Isles who cause unexpected storms and shipwrecks, unless sailors who encounter them can win contests involving rhymes.

Boggarts
A name for a malevolent Scottish male brownie-type fairy in Scotland and the North of England. He also became more

recently known as a hobgoblin after the name lost its original benign associations. In both guises he is blamed for wood decay and the collapse of wooden structures, and for general misfortune to households and farms. In Scotland and the Isle of Man, however, the boggart is synonymous with the bally-bog, a creature of the peat bogs.

Bokwus

Native North American male spirit found near rushing water in spruce forests. Bokwus have entered the folklore of hunters and fishermen, especially in the north-west of America. Distinguished by fierce war paint on their faces, they can seek to drown the unwary.

Brownie

Small brown ragged male fairy who helps around houses and farms, especially in barns and outdoors, in return for a dish of cream and honey. Found in the lore of Scotland, Ireland, the North and Midlands, brownies live in families which suggests there may be females.

Bwca

Welsh brownies who can be unstable in temperament.

Cailleac Bhuer/Blue hag

The Scottish Crone Goddess/deity of winter who walks

through the Highlands in ragged blue or white robes with a crow on her left shoulder and bearing a holly staff.

Cluricaun
Irish male fairy, close kin to the leprechaun, who guards wine cellars especially those of inns. He protects bottles and kegs from being tampered with, leaking or being stolen in return for helping himself to the contents of the cellar. He brings prosperity to inns and private homes with well-stocked cellars, but causes chaos if denied his tribute.

Coblynau
Welsh mine fairies. Like the Cornish knockers, they protect and help miners unless angered.

Corrigan/korrigan
Breton maiden fairy sometimes associated with former pagan princesses or Druidesses who were beautiful by night, but hideous by day. They live near sacred fountains, in grottoes and in woodland groves.

Cururipur
A South American spirit of rain forest and jungle who is guardian of wild creatures, especially tortoises, whom he protects from hunters.

Deva

Nature spirit of a high order who brings healing and coun-
selling to those sensitive enough to hear. Often seen as
golden auras around plants, devas endow plants with healing
properties and aromas and oversee the natural world and its
elemental forces.

Djinn/jinn

The djinn or jinn are invisible, shape-shifting creatures of fire
and air, originating in the Middle East. In Islamic tradition,
djinn live on Earth in a parallel universe and so are invisible
– created, it is said, before mortals from smokeless fire.

They are best known as genies in stories such as *Aladdin*,
and will grant wishes to those who command them. Kept in
bottles or oil lamps to be summoned by their masters, who
were either potentates or master magicians, they were
dangerous servants able to travel almost with the speed of
light, but bringing destruction to any who tried to abuse
their power. Often they would only grant a limited number
of wishes that needed to be phrased carefully, as the genie
would bring what was asked for literally.

Because of their shape-shifting abilities, djinn have been
associated in recent years with some extra-terrestrial
encounters, explicable as meetings with these spirits in one
of their stranger manifestations.

Domovoi

Male Russian elves who, in modern times, often live in

apartments. The females are called *domovikha*. Dolya is a tiny old fairy lady who lives behind the stove and brings good fortune.

Dryad
Female tree nymph, so named in Ancient Greece and associated specifically with the willow (the tree of the moon), oak and ash. Hamadryads remain within the same tree, especially oaks, and die if it is cut down.

Duendes
Spanish, Mexican and South American house spirits who are hostile to human inhabitants. They look like small middle-aged women dressed in green who poke and prod inhabitants with their long fingers during the night.

Duergar
Malicious French and northern English dwarves who guard the ancient fairy paths and can be malevolent to travellers. Dressed in lamb and mole skin, they are blamed for removing signposts or turning them round the wrong way.

Dwarves
Associated with Germany, Scandinavia and Switzerland, dwarves are male, small, wrinkled and grey-bearded even when young. They mine and jealously guard gems and

minerals and are famed for forging magical weapons. They must avoid sunlight or they will be turned to stone.

Ekimmu
An ancient Assyrian spirit who, like the banshee, wails before a death and can wreak vengeance on those who commit murder.

Ellyllon
Tiny ethereal Welsh and Cornish fairies who live near and beneath inland lakes, especially those associated with Lady of the Lake legends; they are her followers.

Elves
Though elves have been recorded worldwide, the most famous are the Scandinavian and German elves, known for spinning and as cobblers. Those who live in troops have kings and queens and are skilled in magic. In England the term elves is used especially for small, mischievous fairy boys, while in Scotland Fairyland is called Elfhame and elves are synonymous with fairies of human proportions (see section on fairies and witchcraft in Chapter 8 for a description of the Queen of Elfhame).

Fauns/faunis
In Ancient Rome fauns were spirits of the forest, described

as having horns, the hooves of a goat and a short tail, similar to Greek satyrs. In modern Italy they are the fairies who guard fields and forests. Originally they were the followers of the forest fertility god Faunus who was half man, half goat, similar to Pan.

Fées

In Brittany trooping fairies are called *fées*. Living in tumuli, dolmens, menhirs or forests, they are believed to be the angels who remained neutral during the war in Heaven, but found the gates of Heaven locked.

Fenoderee

A solitary ugly brownie, exiled from the Manx fairies, who is very strong and helps farmers especially at harvest time.

Ferrishyn

The Manx trooping fairies who have neither king nor queen. Small and able to hear every sound made out of doors, they are easily offended and will spread secrets on the wind.

Folletti

Benign female Italian fairies of the air, who shape-shift into butterflies and travel on the wind, sometimes causing dust clouds.

Formorians

The original Irish giants, now regarded as sea monsters with misshapen forms. Able to travel on land when they leave the sea at night, they are the evil alter egos of the Tuatha de Danaan.

Fossegrim

Norwegian water fairies whose forms disappear into mist where their feet should be. Guardians of waterfalls and fjords, they play exquisite harp music, have mesmeric voices which can enchant mortals and are able to change rapidly from male to female.

Fylgiar

Icelandic familiar that each mortal born inside a caul (a membrane) is said to possess as a guardian throughout life, the fylgiar will share the mortal's home and appear just before the person dies to help him or her to the Otherworld. In Native American lore he/she is the totem spirit who guards each individual, taking an animal form and first seen at the time of initiation as an adolescent.

Gans

Mountain spirits of the Apache nation who are invoked in dance, song and night-time rituals for safe journeys and good weather, especially in mountainous regions.

Ghillie dhu
A solitary, sometimes malevolent, tree fairy who lives in birch trees in Scotland, camouflaged by leaves, moss and foliage.

Gianes
Solitary Italian wood elves, famed for their skill in weaving and divination using the movement of the spinning wheel to create images. Mortals sometimes attempt this form of divination, invoking the wisdom of the Gianes.

Gnomes
The archetypal elemental Earth spirit, who may live beneath oak trees, in forests or in caves throughout western and eastern Europe and Scandinavia. They are said to live for a thousand years and follow the traditional peasant way of life, protecting wild animals and caring for trees. The red-capped, brightly dressed ceramic gnome has became a protective symbol in many European gardens.

Goblins
This is a generic name for the small but powerful malevolent fairies who roam in bands and live in dark underground places or deep forests, overpowering by sheer numbers other fairy folk, including dwarves, and making them work as their slaves.

Gremlins

Found in Europe, especially in England and Germany, these hairy brown malevolent mountain-dwellers are incredibly strong and wreak havoc on machines, especially aeroplanes. They do so because, it is said, they once had the ability to fly and so resent mortals who possess their lost power.

Gruagach

A kindly Scottish guardian of grazing animals, leading them to water and guarding sheep and cattle from harm. Ugly and covered in hair, she is always cold and seeks shelter by crofters' fires, rewarding those who do not turn her away.

Gwragedd Annwn

Beautiful, golden-haired, female Welsh water fairies, living in palaces beneath lakes in the Black Mountains. They are kind to children, to those who have no money and to mothers.

Gwyllion

Welsh female mountain fairies who can shape-shift into goats, who are their special animals. Less friendly to mortals, they lure night-time travellers off paths and into danger. They fear storms, iron and sunlight.

Hamadryadniks
Eastern European tree spirits, akin to hamadryads, who disguise themselves as foliage. However, unusually for tree spirits they leave their homes during daylight.

Hill trows
Scottish trolls who live in hollow hills on the Shetland and Orkney Islands. They hate sunlight and are said to try to eat mortals unless they can escape by crossing a stream.

Hobgoblins
Small, wizened creatures without fingers or toes who live in Britain, America and Canada. They have unfairly been branded as evil and were originally benevolent hearth (hob) spirits.

Hu hsien
Malevolent Chinese shape-shifting spirits of nature who are known as fox spirits. They have been seen walking through walls and other solid matter.

Hyldermoder
Scandinavian spirits who live in elder trees, known as Elder-mothers. They are benign to mortals except to those who damage an elder tree.

Hyter sprites

Shape-shifting fairies from eastern England, they most frequently assume the form of birds. Also found in Spain and Mexico, they live in flocks or groups. The connection between East Anglia and Spain is puzzling.

Ieles

Eastern European vampire fairies that appear in the night like huge two-legged cats. Associated with crossroads, traditional places of magical powers, they lure victims with their mesmeric singing.

Jimaninos/jimaninas

These winged nature spirits live in Mexico and Central America, but probably originated from Spain rather than being indigenous. They are said to resemble well-fed children and are most visible on El Dia del Muerte, the Mexican Days of the Dead, 1 and 2 November, especially the latter day, when departed children are remembered.

Kachinas

Among the Native American Hopi these benign spirits, are said to emerge from the Earth at the Winter Solstice. They are represented by either dancers or dolls, painted in the colours of the six cardinal points – in this tradition yellow for the north, red for the south, white for the east, turquoise for the west, black for sky and grey for earth. They remain in the world until after the Summer Solstice and various rituals are performed in their honour, including the False Spring or Powamu bean dance in February. The kachinas are especially concerned with young people and initiation into their Earth Walk as adults. A few kachinas, called the two-hearted, are harsh to those who fail in their ceremonial and social obligations.

Kappa
These are malevolent water spirits in Japan who attack swimmers and fisher folk in remote lakes and rivers.

Kelpies
Scottish, long-fanged water demons who are expert shape-shifters, associated with Scottish lochs especially Loch Ness. They are sometimes described as water horses who lure riders and then drag them beneath the waters; and are also known to appear as handsome youths except for their seaweed hair.

Knockers
Dwarf-like Cornish mine fairies who are left tributes of food and drink by miners and in return warn of danger or draw the miners to seams of ore by making tapping sounds.

Korrs/Korreds

Male Breton elves with huge heads and spiky hair who guard ancient stones and stone circles in Brittany. Believed to have created the sacred sites, they frighten away those who would desecrate the stones. Unfortunately in Carnac, one of the major Breton megalithic sites, the stone rows are currently fenced off as the Korrs were unable to stop the natural erosion caused by so many pilgrims and visitors. Unusually for fairies, they do not fear iron.

Kul

Inuit water spirit who helps fishermen find the shoals and protects them. He can be unpredictable, reflecting the wildness of the Arctic seas, and so is offered the first fish of the season.

Leprechauns

Irish fairy shoemakers, dressed in green with tricorn hats. They are solitary because they guard ancient treasure which they hide in crocks. It can be revealed but rarely captured – the elusive end of the rainbow invariably shines over one of these hiding places. The name was originally only used in the north Leinster area.

Linchetti

Italian elves who emerge at night. They dislike disorder in their surroundings and may bring nightmares to those who offend them.

Lorelei

Akin to the Sirens of Greek myth, the term is now a generic one for female water sprites in Europe, especially those of fresh water sources, whose beautiful voices lure sailors to their doom.

Lunantishess/Lunantisidhe

Irish blackthorn fairies who protect the trees. No blackthorn stick, used for making the Irish walking stick/protective weapon known as a shillelagh, may be cut from a living tree on 11 November, the Day of the Dead in the old Julian calendar, or 11 May, the original May Day. The blackthorn fairies worship the Moon Goddess.

Lutins

Breton shape-shifting fairies associated mainly with homes, though occasionally living close to water. In the domestic setting he or she expected tribute and consideration or would become spiteful and destructive. There was, for example, a custom of cooling used cooking pans with water so that the lutin would not get burned.

Manitou

Antlered fairies, indigenous to the Algonquin tribe in eastern North America, whose drumming could be heard miles away. They are said to practise drum magic.

Matka Syra Ziemia

Slavic name for Mother Earth. No one could strike the earth with a hoe before the Spring Equinox for fear of disturbing her pregnancy.

Mazikeen

Winged Jewish fairies who were the offspring of Adam and Eve after the Fall and were created from their union with spirits. Expert shape-shifters, known also as *shideem*, they are skilled in all magical arts and as seers.

Merrows

Irish sea people who are distinguishable from other mer people because they wear red feather caps that transport them beneath the waves. As with the selkies' sealskins, without their caps merrows were condemned to live on land. Female merrows are beautiful, but the males very ugly.

Mimis

Slender, long-limbed, indigenous Australian rock spirits, living in the northern hills. They inhabit crevices and fear wind because it can blow them away, so they emerge only for food – reputed occasionally to be mortals lost in the hills.

Moors

Portuguese fairies who live in the rocky hills above rivers

and underground in palaces. They are most powerful on the night of the full moon, when their mesmeric singing would be heard and humans feared they would take away their children. Moors disguised as old women would occasionally knock on doors and, if admitted, might enchant children who would be identified by a crescent moon beneath the arm.

Moss people

German and Swiss woodland spirits with huge butterfly wings, known also in their female form as moss wives, who inhabit the ancient woodlands, though like many tree spirits they can merge into the foliage and moss. The moss women can be quite wild if confronted.

Nagas

In Hindu myth creatures of earth and water, a primeval race of divine serpent-people who bring rain and so, in a hot land, fertility. Nagas live in palaces in an underground city and on one hand are protectors of springs, wells and rivers, but on the other are blamed for disasters such as floods and drought.

Nunnehi

Perhaps the most historically fascinating of the Native North American indigenous fairies. Associated with the Cherokees, they are believed to have guided the nation to safety during the sorrowful time when they were being moved from their homelands to the resettlement areas.

Nymphs

Generic terms for earth and water spirits, who were first recorded in the tales of Ancient Greece. They include dryads, who were spirits of the trees, naiads from springs and rivers, and oceanids from the sea. Because of their great beauty and gentleness they frequently became the lovers of deities, heroes and mortals, and so were unfairly associated with unwise passion.

Pechs/Pehts

Scottish Lowland fairies, associated with the Picts, they built ancient stone towers and castles and lived in round houses beneath the earth. They emerge only at night – perhaps, therefore, a folk memory of the small Pictish peoples who were conquered by tall iron-wielding invaders.

Penates/Lares

In Ancient Rome the Lares and Penates presided over dwellings and the affairs of the household. The Lares were deified ancestors or heroes and the *lar familiaris* was the spirit of the founder of the house, who never left it. The Penates were chiefly the gods of the storeroom and guardians of the home, who protected all within from external danger. Their statues had a corner of honour in each house and wine, incense, cakes and honey were offered at family festivities.

Phookas

Black shape-shifting goblins from Ireland who live as wild bands of brigands. They can assume many forms, including bulls and wild dogs, but most frequently shape-shift as a pony that will take an unwary traveller on a terrifying ride and eventually throw the rider into the mud.

Pixies

Small, dark, winged Cornish elves, once said to be Picts who have continued to diminish in size. In Cornwall there are said to be two kinds of pixies: those who live on land and those who make their homes close to the sea between the high and low water marks of the tide. The latter, sometimes called Buccas, were traditionally offered some of a fisherman's catch as tribute.

Rozhinitsy

Slavic mother and daughter Fates, dual-nature spirits are common in Slavic mythology, for example the Zorya – goddesses of dusk and dawn.

Red caps

So called because of their brilliant red caps, these very

malevolent Scottish and Irish elf-like fairies haunt ruined castles and towers. The red cap has blazing red eyes, a grey beard and the claws of an eagle and wears iron boots, so breaking the fairy taboo of iron.

Salamanders

These are the elemental spirits of Fire, from the Middle East. Described as fire lizards, salamanders live in volcanoes or lakes of fire.

Satyrs

Ancient Greek male forest spirits with the legs and tail of a goat, though the Greek sculptor Praxiteles portrayed the satyr as more human than animal.

Selkies

Water fairies who wear sealskins. The females are beautiful, the males ugly, and they create storms to deter seal hunters.

Spriggans

Ugly bands of fairies living in Ireland who can instantly increase in size and wreak havoc on crops, animals, property and sometimes humans.

Sylphs
The elemental winged Air spirits, who live hundreds of years and can, it is said, attain an immortal soul through good deeds.

Tengu
Japanese winged woodland fairies who carry fans made of feathers. They may shape-shift, especially into woodland animals, but have little contact with mortals.

Tokolush
Southern African spirits who resemble baboons with long black hair. Dwelling near streams, they try to frighten travellers.

Tomtra
A male brownie of uncertain temperament living in Finland. Famed for playing the fiddle, he will stay only in the most immaculate of homes.

Torngak
The name comes from Torngasak, the spirit who is called the Good Being by Inuits. Torngasak himself is often depicted as a bear. Every natural form including the animals and the sea itself has an *innua* or spirit. Such forces sometimes assume the role of Torngak, becoming guardians of individual Inuits.

Trolls

Mainly of Germanic and Scandinavian origin, trolls have ugly, fleshy faces and a profusion of hair on their feet, hands and heads. Varying in size from huge ogre-type creatures to quite small forest dwellers, they are the traditional guardians of bridges and highways but often live in kingdoms in underground caverns.

Tylwyth Teg

Known as the Fair Family in Wales and also as Bendith Y Mammau, Mothers' Blessing, they live either beneath lakes, on fairy islands or underground in beautiful palaces. The Gwragedd Annwn of the Black Mountains are a localised form.

Undines

Small Ancient Greek water spirits from the Aegean Sea, said to resemble sea horses in the water. They are the creatures of the Water element in magic and alchemy.

Yumboes

Silver-haired fairies from Senegal in West Africa who hold revels by moonlight. Their homes are exotic palaces beneath the hills.

Suggested Reading

Some of the older books are well worth searching out, whether from New Age shops with good secondhand departments, old bookshops or sometimes as online editions.

Anderson, Rosemarie, *Celtic Oracles* (Piatkus, 1999)

Balfour, Michael, *Megalithic Mysteries* (Dragon's World, 1996)

Bettelheim, B., *The Uses of Enchantment: The Meaning and Importance of Fairy Tales* (Vintage Books, New York, 1975)

Blavatsky, Helena, *The Secret Doctrine: The Synthesis of Science, Religion and Philosophy* (Theosophical University Press, 1992)

Bloom, William, *Working with Angels, Fairies and Nature Spirits* (Piatkus, 1998)

Bord, Janet, *Fairies – Real Encounters with Little People* (Michael O'Mara, 1997)

Briggs, Katherine, *The Fairies in English Tradition and Literature* (Routledge and Kegan Paul, 1967)

Briggs, Katherine, *The Vanishing People* (Pantheon Books, 1978)

Brooksmith, Peter and Paul Devereux, *UFOs and UFOlogy* (Blandford, 1997)

Cooper, Joe, *The Cottingley Fairies* (Simon and Schuster, 1998)

Cross, T. P. and C. H. Slover, *Ancient Irish Tales* (Barnes and Noble, 1996)

Crowley, Vivienne, *Wicca: The Old Religion in the New Age* (Aquarian, Thorsons, 1989)

Cunningham, Scott, *Complete Book of Oils, Incenses and Brews* (Llewellyn, St Paul, Minnesota, 1991)

Cunningham, Scott, *Encyclopedia of Crystal, Gem and Metal Magic* (Llewellyn, St Paul, Minnesota, 1991)

Devereux, Paul, *Earthlights Revelation, UFOs and Mystery Lightform Phenomena: The Earth's Secret Energy Force* (Blandford, 1989)

Eason, Cassandra, *Psychic Power of Children* (Foulsham, 1994)

Eason, Cassandra, *A Complete Guide to Magic and Ritual* (Piatkus, 1999)

Eason, Cassandra, *Pendulum Dowsing* (Piatkus, 1999)

Eason, Cassandra, *Crystals Talk to the Woman Within* (Quantum/Foulsham, 2000)

Evans-Wentz, W. Y., *The Fairy Faith in Celtic Countries* (Lemma, New York, 1973)

Fortune, Dion, *The Goat-foot God* (Aquarian, 1989)

Graves, Robert, *The White Goddess* (Faber & Faber, 1961)

Green, Miranda, *Dictionary of Celtic Myth and Legend* (Thames and Hudson, 1992)

Jung, Emma and Marie Louise von Franz, *The Grail Legend* (Element, 1989)

Kirk, Robert (ed. Andrew Lang), *The Secret Commonwealth of*

Elves, Fauns and Fairies (Eneas Mackay, 1893; 1933 edn)

Matthews, Caitlin and John, *The Encyclopaedia of Celtic Wisdom* (Element, 1994)

Mitchell, Kathleen, *The Handbook of Witches* (Arthur Baker, 1965)

Murray, Margaret, *The God of the Witches* (Faber & Faber, 1931)

Opie, Iona and Peter, *The Classical Fairy Tales* (Paladin, 1974)

Randles, Jenny, *The Complete Book of Aliens and Abductions* (Piatkus, 2000)

Starhawk, *The Spiral Dance* (Harper & Row, San Francisco, 1999)

Stewart, R. J., *The Prophetic Vision of Merlin* (Arkana, Penguin, 1986)

Sullivan, Brian, *Ley Lines* (Piatkus, 2000)

Thomas, Keith, *Religion and the Decline of Magic* (Penguin, 1991)

Tompkins, Peter and Christopher Bird, *Secret Life of Plants* (Avon Books, New York, 1974)

Van-Gelder, Dora, *The Real World of Fairies* (Theosophical Publishing House, 1977)

Watkins, Alfred, *The Old Straight Track* (Abacus, 1974)

Yeats, W. B., *Fairy and Folk Tales of Ireland* (Collier Books, 1986)

Zimmer, Bradley Marion, *Mists of Avalon* (Penguin, 1984)

Zipes, J., *Fairy Tale as Myth, Myth as Fairy Tale* (Ballantine Books, New York, 2000)

Useful
Addresses

Fairy Collectables and Books

Australia
G & M Treasures
PO Box 133
Kippas
ACT 2615
Fantasy figures, pewter figurines.

Glass Designs P/L
PO Box 340
Byron Bay
NSW 2481
Flower fairies, fairy figurines and collectables.

UK
The Faerie Shop Ltd
105 High Street
Marlborough
Wiltshire
SN8 1LT

Tel: 01672 515995

3 Montpelier Walk
Cheltenham
Gloucestershire
GL50 1SD

Tel: 01242 230833

6 Lower Borough Walls
Bath
Avon
BA1 1QR
All things fairy. A good first port of call.

Tel: 01225 427773

Mother Goose
West Green House
Upper Green Road
St Helens
Isle of Wight
PO33 1VB
Flower fairies and antiquarian and first edition modern books, including fairy tales.

Snapdragon
12 South Park
Sevenoaks
Kent
TN13 1AW
All kinds of fairy collectables, dragons etc.

USA
Continental Collectibles
PMB 1141
22833 Bothell-Everett Highway
Bothell
WA 98021
Flower fairies.

The Fairy Company
1186 Cielo Circle
Rohnert Park
CA 94928
All kinds of fairy items.

Tel: 707-664-0476
Fax: 707-795-0635
Email: malia@fairycompany.com
Website: www.fairycompany.com

Light as a Feather
Eric Torgeson
216 Palisade Drive
Eureka Springs
Arizona 72631
Hand sculptured glass fairies. Light as a feather fairies, are created exclusively by Eric Torgeson. The collection has grown to well over three thousand possible combinations of pairing and colour.

Joyce Wiseman
PO Box 333
Comptche
CA 95427
Mermaids, fairy dolls, mermaid and fairy cards.

EARTH ENERGIES

Australia
Dowsers Society of New South Wales
c/o Mrs E. Miksevicius
126 Fiddens Wharf Road
Killara
NSW 2031

Southern Tasmania Dowsing Association
PO Box 101
Moonah
Tasmania 7009

UK
British Society of Dowsers
Sycamore Barn
Hastingleigh
Ashford
Kent
TN25 5HW

Tel/Fax: (+44) (0)1233 750253
Email: bsd@dowsers.demon.co.uk
Website: www.britishdowsers.org

Findhorn Foundation
The Park
Forres
Scotland
IV36 3TX
Workshops and courses that teach about meditation, consciousness and nature spirits.

Tel: 01309 690311

USA
The American Society of Dowsers
Dowsers Hall
Danville
Vermont 05828-0024

Tel: (+1) 802 684 3417 or (+1) 800 711 9530
Email: asd@dowsers.org
Website: www.dowsers.org

CRYSTALS, CANDLES, MAGICAL SUPPLIES

Australia
Future Pastimes
24a Collins St
Kiama
New South Wales
General supplies. Mail order.

The Mystic Trader
125 Flinders Lane
Melbourne 3000
Mail order as well as personal service.

Mysterys
Level 1
314–322 Darling Street
Balmain
New South Wales
Wiccan supplies. Mail order.

South Africa
The Wellstead
1 Wellington Avenue
Wynberg
Cape 7300
Mail order.

UK
Futhark
18 Halifax Road
Todmorden
Lancs
OL14 5AD
Occult, magical and alchemical supplies of all kinds. Mail order.

Mandragora
Essex House
Thame
OX9 3LS
Mail order.

Mysteries
7 Monmouth Street
London
WC2H 9DA

Mysteries Ltd
9–11 Monmouth St
London
WC2H 9DA
Shop/mail order, absolutely everything for the New Age, plus good advice.

Tel: (+44) (0)20 7240 3688

Pentagram
16 The Springs
Wakefield
West Yorkshire
WF1 1QE
Mail order and personal, everything for the New Age, Wiccan and occult.

Tel: 01924 298930

USA
Eye of the Cat
3314 E Broadway
Long Beach
CA 90803
Mail order crystals and other New Age commodities.

The Crystal Cave
415 West Foothill Blvd
Claremont
CA 91711
Mail order. Stocks a huge variety of crystal and stones including unusual ones.

Open Door Metaphysical Shoppe
428 North Buchanan Circle
Suite 16
Pacheco
California 94553
Mail order.

Spirit Search Emporium
Sun Angel Innovations
3939 W Windmills Blvd
2060 Chandler
Arizona 85226
Mail order.

FLOWER/TREE ESSENCES – SUPPLIERS AND COURSES

Australia
The Australian Flower Remedy Society
PO Box 531
Spit Junction
New South Wales 2007

Contact:
Sabian
PO Box 527
Kew
Victoria 3101

or

The Sabian Centre
11 Selbourne Road
Kew
Victoria 31031

Bush Flower Essences
8a Oaks Avenue
Dee Why
NSW 2099
Australia

(+61) 29 972 1033

UK
Bach Flower Remedies
Dr Edward Bach Ltd
Mount Vernon
Bakers Lane
Sotwell
Wallingford
OX10 0PZ

Tel: (+44) (0)1491 825022
Fax: (+44) (0)1491 834678
www.bachcentre.com

USA
Alaskan Flower Essence Project
PO Box 1329
Homer
AL 99603

Tel: (+1) 907 235 2188

Desert Alchemy
PO Box 44189
Tucson
AZ 85733

Pacific Essences
PO Box 8317
Victoria
BC V8W 3R9

PAGANISM

Australia
Novocastrian Pagan Information Centre
Laren
PO Box 129
Stockton
New South Wales 2295

The Pagan Alliance
PO Box 823
Bathurst
New South Wales 2795
An umbrella movement for pagan organisations.

UK
The Pagan Federation
BM Box 7097
London
WC1N 3XX

TOOTH FAIRIES

USA
Tooth Fairy Museum
1129 Deerfield Cherry Street
Illinois
Tooth fairy drawings can be sent to PO Box 7196, Deerfield,
Illinois 60015.

WICCA/GODDESS ORGANISATIONS

Ireland
Fellowship of Isis
Huntington Castle
Bunclody
Enniscorthy
Eire
A worldwide network of goddess worshippers.

USA
Circle Sanctuary
PO Box 219
Mount Horeb
WI 53572
Contacts with seven hundred pagan groups, networks etc.

Tel: (+1) 608 924 2216

Covenant of the Goddess
PO Box 1226
Berkeley
California
94704

The Witches' Voice Inc
PO Box 4924
Clearwater
Florida 33758-4924
A resource organisation with worldwide links.

Cassandra Eason's website is www.cassandraeason.co.uk

Index